Claiming Space

Claiming Space

Performing the Personal through Decorated Mortarboards

Sheila Bock

Volume 5
Ritual, Festival, and Celebration
A series edited by Jack Santino

Utah State University Press
Logan

Published by Utah State University Press
An imprint of University Press of Colorado
1580 North Logan Street, Suite 660
PMB 39883
Denver, Colorado 80203-1942

 ASSOCIATION of UNIVERSITY PRESSES

The University Press of Colorado is a proud member of
the Association of University Presses.

The University Press of Colorado is a cooperative publishing enterprise supported, in part, by Adams State University, Colorado State University, Fort Lewis College, Metropolitan State University of Denver, University of Alaska Fairbanks, University of Colorado, University of Denver, University of Northern Colorado, University of Wyoming, Utah State University, and Western Colorado University.

∞ This paper meets the requirements of the ANSI/NISO Z39.48-1992 (Permanence of Paper).

ISBN: 978-1-64642-523-5 (hardcover)
ISBN: 978-1-64642-524-2 (paperback)
ISBN: 978-1-64642-525-9 (ebook)
https://doi.org/10.7330/9781646425259

Library of Congress Cataloging-in-Publication Data

Names: Bock, Sheila Marie, author.
Title: Claiming space : performing the personal through decorated mortarboards / Sheila Bock.
Description: Logan : Utah State University Press, [2023] | Includes bibliographical references and index.
Identifiers: LCCN 2023020617 (print) | LCCN 2023020618 (ebook) | ISBN 9781646425235 (hardcover) | ISBN 9781646425242 (paperback) | ISBN 9781646425259 (ebook)
Subjects: LCSH: Academic costume—Social aspects—United States. | Commencement ceremonies—Social aspects—United States. | Academic achievement—Social aspects—United States. | Education, Higher—Aims and objectives—United States. | Degrees, Academic—United States—Psychological aspects. | College graduates—United States—Attitudes. | Universities and colleges—United States—Sociological aspects.
Classification: LCC LB2389 .B64 2023(print) | LCC LB2389(ebook) | DDC 378.2/8—dc23/eng/20230519
LC record available at https://lccn.loc.gov/2023020617
LC ebook record available at https://lccn.loc.gov/2023020618

To my parents, Fran and Russ Bock, for their ongoing, unwavering love and support.

Contents

List of Figures   ix

Acknowledgments   xi

1.   Introduction   3

2.   Crafting Performances of Self   30

3.   Dress and the Visual Rhetorics of Belonging and Exclusion in the Commencement Ritual   63

4.   Into the Public Sphere: Countering, Rearticulating, and Reimagining Dominant Narratives of Citizenship   79

5.   Undisciplining Graduation   96

6.   Conclusion: A Brief Reflection on Trivial Matters   111

Notes   121

References   127

Index   137

About the Author   145

Figures

1.1.   Decorated mortarboards are both informed by and responsive to broader discourses about the value of higher education in the United States.   7

1.2.   Decorated mortarboards have become such an established expressive genre that common generic features are playfully referenced in the designs themselves.   16

1.3.   Through their language and imagery, caps can be transformed into overt sites of political expression.   19

1.4.   Decorated mortarboards can work to position the graduate in relation to broader identity categories.   19

1.5.   Individuals often decorate mortarboards in ways that visibly mark important relationships in their lives.   21

1.6.   Decorated mortarboards can mark meaningful human–animal relationships.   22

1.7.   Graduates often use the space of the mortarboard to highlight aspects of their identity and experiences that extend beyond their role as a student.   26

1.8.   Sometimes elements of the mortarboard's design are selected with the intention of offering implicit critiques of the university setting.   27

2.1.   Like scrapbooks, another material genre of personal expression, mortarboard displays curate an assemblage of discrete textual, visual, and material forms that carry significant meanings for the graduate.   36

2.2.   Decorated mortarboards are complex, multimodal performances of self that can reference multiple personal experiences and perspectives at the same time.   40

2.3.   Graduates often use media texts as discursive resources in their crafted presentations of self.   42

2.4.   The image macro is a digital folklore genre that is commonly integrated into the mortarboard designs.   43

2.5.   Some graduates use the space of the mortarboard to highlight, and thus "remain true" to, aspects of the self that may at first glance seem at odds with the persona of the successful student.   48

2.6.   Dress is a powerful form of communication, and the meanings carried by different forms of dress and bodily adornment (in this case, a military dog tag and fatigues) are often integrated into the designs of decorated mortarboards.   50

2.7.   Facing the challenge of deciding what elements of the self to put on display, some graduates opt to decorate two mortarboards: one to wear for the commencement ceremony and one to wear for pictures to post on social media.   55

2.8.   Utilized as sites of strategic visibility, graduation caps create opportunities
        to engage in destigmatization and to be a source of affirmation and
        solidarity for those who have had similar experiences.   57

3.1.   Attention to hair by many Black graduates, both under and on top of the
        graduation caps, offers just one example of graduates' engagement with a
        broader politics of visibility in the space of commencement.   75

3.2.   Many graduates, particularly graduates who have felt marginalized in
        the university setting, understand their visible presence in the space of
        commencement to be an act of resistance.   77

4.1.   Many decorated caps position graduates as DREAMers, individuals who
        arrived in the United States as minors and consequently do not have US
        citizenship.   82

4.2.   Mortarboards highlighting dichos such as this one can work to challenge
        deficit models that situate cultural ways of knowing as being at odds with
        academic achievement.   87

4.3.   Integrating flag imagery into the designs of decorated mortarboards is one
        way graduates position themselves in relation to different national identities
        and cultural heritages.   90

4.4.   Mortarboard displays such as this one explicitly link the personal and the
        political.   91

4.5.   Cultural references ranging from folk traditions to popular culture serve as
        rich discursive resources, invoking shared community experiences while also
        disrupting the conflation between assimilation and belonging.   93

5.1.   Engaging with themes such as debt and financial hardship, playful
        mortarboard designs can inspire ambivalent laughter.   97

5.2.   Graduation caps commonly feature the notion of forward momentum with
        a clear orientation toward the future.   99

5.3.   Graduation caps can become sites for reenvisioning the disciplining logics
        of "straight time."   103

5.4.   Graduation caps often become a tangible space where the tactics of student
        life are put on display.   107

5.5.   Many decorated mortarboards reference graduates' anxieties and
        ambivalence about an increasingly precarious future.   109

6.1.   Like the seemingly trivial marginalia in medieval ecclesiastical texts,
        decorated mortarboards help shape the meaning of the commencement as
        a whole.   112

Acknowledgments

FACED WITH THE DAUNTING (AND I DARESAY IMPOSSIBLE) task of properly acknowledging everyone who played a role in helping this book come to be, I must begin with the students. I owe special thanks to all of the graduates, both from University of Nevada, Las Vegas (UNLV) and elsewhere, who shared their personal experiences with the expressive tradition of decorating mortarboards. Their generosity with both their time and their insights made this book possible.

My critical engagement with the broader discourses surrounding higher education was heavily informed by the honest and thoughtful reflections the UNLV students in my Interdisciplinary Studies classes shared in class discussions, written assignments, and individual conversations. UNLV students Claudia Chiang-López, Brenda Carolina Cruz Gomez, Jaqueline Eddy, Nicole Cristina Espinosa, Sofia Molina Gallardo, Jaqueline Kupovits, and Alissia Medina played an integral role in helping me document this tradition, taking photographs and conducting interviews at UNLV's commencement ceremonies in May 2017, December 2017, May 2018, and December 2018. I am also grateful for the invitations to speak about this research for undergraduate folklore courses at The Ohio State University and Utah State University, where I received questions from students that deepened my thinking about different aspects of this creative tradition.

In its very early stages, as my ideas were just beginning to take form, this project benefited greatly from conversations with Paddy Bowman, Danille Christensen, Desiré Galvez, Rachel González-Martin, Rosemary Hathaway, Molly McBride, Lynne McNeill, Lisa Rathje, and Christina Xydias. The support of Cassie Rosita Patterson, who was then associate director and director of the Folklore Archives at The Ohio State University Center for Folklore Studies, was particularly influential, leading to the creation of the #GradCapTraditions archival collection, where many of the materials collected for this project have been digitally archived. Sarah Craycraft, Jordan Lovejoy, and Afsane

Rezaei, graduate students working for the Center for Folklore Studies, also made valuable contributions to the #GradCapTraditions project.

As preliminary ideas eventually took the form of (often messy) written pages, Kate Parker Horigan, Norma Marrun, Cassie Rosita Patterson, and Martha Sims generously served as the first readers of various pieces of this book, offering key feedback that undoubtedly strengthened the work as a whole. I also gave presentations on this work in progress at the annual meetings of the American Folklore Society, the Western States Folklore Society, and the Far West Popular Culture Association, where I received both encouragement and helpful suggestions along the way.

Parts of the introduction were previously published in 2014 in "Performing the Personal in a State of Transition: Decorated Mortarboards" in the *Journal of Folklore and Education*. They are reprinted here courtesy of the *Journal of Folklore and Education*, https://JFEPublications.org, a publication of Local Learning: The National Network for Folk Arts in Education. An earlier version of chapter 4 was previously published in "#LatinxGradCaps, Cultural Citizenship, and the 'American Dream'" in *Folklore and Social Media*.

I thank Julie Long for her transcription services. I am also indebted to Rachael Levay of the University Press of Colorado for her shepherding of this project through the publication process, and for the feedback of the two anonymous reviewers.

I owe great thanks to the support structures I have found during my time at UNLV. My early documentation work was supported by funding from the College of Liberal Arts in 2017, and I had the opportunity to give focused attention to this project during a sabbatical in fall 2018. The College of Liberal Arts also provided additional subvention funding to support the publication of this book. I am exceedingly grateful to my colleagues in the Department of Interdisciplinary, Gender, and Ethnic Studies, whose support has manifested in both big and small ways that extend well beyond the scope of this project: Erika Abad, Marian Anderson, Constancio Arnaldo, Jessica Bradley, Manoucheka Celeste, Lynn Comella, Millicent Fila, Kendra Gage, Tim Gauthier, Javon Johnson, Stacy Macías, Brandon Manning, Caitlin Moscato, Mark Padoongpatt, Tyler Parry, Laurence Reese, Anita Revilla Tijerina, Danielle Roth-Johnson, Sreshtha Sen, Anne Stevens, Valerie Taylor, and Pam Weiss. My time at UNLV has been further enriched by my interactions with friends and colleagues outside of my department, including Christie Batson, Emma Bloomfield, Kaitlin Clinnin, Andy Cummings, John Curry, Carlos Dimas, Liam Frink, Noelle Lefforge, Norma Marrun, Miriam Melton-Villanueva, Jeff Schauer, Michelle Tusan, Tessa Winkelmann, and Gloria Wong-Padoongpatt.

I am indebted to my teachers and mentors in the field of folklore studies, from Alan Dundes, who introduced me to the field when I was an undergraduate student at the University of California, Berkeley, to Dorothy Noyes, who served as the advisor for my dissertation at The Ohio State University and remains a consistent supporter and good friend over a decade later. Others who have played a formative role in my development as a folklorist, who have shaped the "folkloristic eye" I use to view the world around me, include Amy Shuman, Katherine Borland, Sabra Webber, Diane Goldstein, Barbara Lloyd, Tim Lloyd, and Patrick Mullen.

I continue to be grateful for friendships that have been sustained through geographical distance and ever-evolving life circumstances with affection, support, and humor: Kelly Bradbury, Beth Coggeshall, Katie Comer, Ann Ferrell, Kirsi Hänninen, Kate Parker Horigan, Mike Juneau, Jennifer Kawahara, Dana Lee, Chris Levonian, Helen Liu, Ashley Overstreet, Cassie Rosita Patterson, Elo-Hanna Seljamaa, Martha Sims, and Nancy Yan. I am also grateful for the friendship of Amy Ayoub, my next-door neighbor and one of the first people I met when I moved to Las Vegas, who took it upon herself to make my husband and I love our new city as much as she did, and in the process became an important part of our family (ultimately taking on the role of honorary grandmother to our two children). In addition, I have much gratitude for Tamara Bock, my first friend, my best friend, and my big sister whose quests to find and make beauty in the everyday continue to inspire.

I owe a great deal of thanks to my sons, MJ and Tommy, for reminding me of the importance of putting things into perspective and making time for play. I am a better person for it.

My husband, Michael Alarid, has been hands down the biggest supporter of this project. Indeed, he realized it should become a book before I did, and he was a consistent source of encouragement when I had my doubts. I am thankful for his dedication to our family, his phenomenal cooking skills, and his love.

And finally, I extend my deepest appreciation to my parents, Fran and Russ Bock, to whom this book is dedicated, for their unconditional love, their unwavering support, and their enthusiastic love of learning that they passed along to me.

Claiming Space

1

Introduction

"WHAT GOOD IS OUR EDUCATION NOW?"

In December 2011, I attended the commencement ceremony at the University of Nevada, Las Vegas (UNLV), where I had just completed my first semester as a new faculty member. I wore the same black puffy velvet tam and red doctoral robe—embellished with gray velvet and long, bell-shaped sleeves—I wore the year before when I completed my PhD and attended my own commencement at The Ohio State University. Before the ceremony began, I stood in line with other faculty members dressed in similar robes, though in different colors depending on where they earned their degrees, and when the music began, we started the multicolored faculty procession into the large arena where the ceremony was taking place. Proceeding through the center of the arena while thousands of people in the audience looked on, we eventually sat down in the first few rows next to the stage. The procession of graduating students soon followed, along with the loud applause that erupted as friends and families of the graduates began to cheer for their loved ones. The doctoral candidates came first and sat in the rows directly behind the faculty, dressed in the same style of robes the faculty wore, though theirs were gray with red embellishment to signify the school colors of UNLV. Later on, during a special hooding ceremony on the stage, each individual's dress ensemble would grow to include a doctoral hood, which would be placed around their neck by their academic advisor, a visual and embodied marker of their change in status from student to holder of a doctoral degree. After the doctoral candidates came the master's degree candidates, who wore a master's hood around their neck, along with a simpler black robe with shorter pointed sleeves, and a flat, four-sided cap on their heads. The final group to join the procession were the graduates earning their under-graduate degrees, wearing the same style of cap and gown as the master's degree candidates but in red.

https://doi.org/10.7330/9781646425259.c001

The ceremony that followed included the presentation of colors by the UNLV Air Force and Army ROTC Honor Guards, a student's performance of the national anthem, a performance of the UNLV Alma Mater by the UNLV Choral Ensemble, the recognition of outstanding graduates, and speeches by the university president and two preselected student speakers. It culminated in the conferral of degrees. At this point in the ceremony, from my vantage point sitting toward the front of the arena, I watched excited graduates file past me so that they could walk across the stage, wave to family and friends in the audience, and shake hands with a representative of the university to ritually mark the completion of their degree. I also quickly began to notice that many of these graduates had decorated the flat, four-sided caps—or mortarboards—that sat atop their heads.

I delighted in the creative, sometimes silly, often poignant messages and modes of artistic display I observed through these material sites of expression. At the same time, I was struck by how prevalent the practice has become. Up until this point, I was not wholly unfamiliar with embellished mortarboards. For example, during my own undergraduate commencement in 2003 at University of California, Berkeley, I remember that some graduates did decorate their caps, but it was certainly not the norm.[1] Sitting in that arena at UNLV in 2011, I found that while not all the graduates had embellished their mortarboards, those who did were no longer the outliers. Indeed, decorating one's graduation cap had become a well-established and widespread practice.

Social media platforms such as Pinterest, Instagram, Twitter, Tumblr, and Facebook have undoubtedly contributed to the popularity of the practice at institutions of higher education across the country, not just at UNLV, as students no longer need to attend commencement ceremonies in person or know graduates personally to see examples of decorated mortarboards. Indeed, in my conversations with college graduates while working on this book, most have identified these social media platforms as the sites where they learned about the practice of decorating mortarboards in the first place. The mortarboards themselves, in the words of one graduate I talked to, are very "Instagrammable," meaning that they are visually appealing, easy to photograph, and easy to share. They also fit well with the goals of social media platforms like Instagram, a social networking application typically used for curating one's digital self through the sharing of photos representing personal perspectives and experiences with friends and followers. As more and more people have posted photos of their decorated mortarboards online, and as these photos have been shared by others, individual decorated mortarboards have found much larger audiences than they have had in the past, which in turn has inspired others to decorate their own.

Universities are also becoming more amenable to students' adaptations of the ritual dress of commencement. Educational institutions have not always been receptive to graduates' modifications of the traditional academic dress and even today some educational institutions (particularly at the high school level) actively prohibit them. Others embrace them. Some universities launch contests where students can vote for which graduate has the best mortarboard display or host events on campus for students to decorate their mortarboards, providing free food and art supplies. During graduation seasons, university webpages and alumni magazines often feature images of caps proclaiming messages of celebration and school spirit, highlighting individual messages that align with institutional branding. Against this backdrop, each year all over the country, as graduating seniors obtain their caps, gowns, and honor cords in preparation for the pomp and circumstance of commencement ceremonies, many choose to participate in the practice of decorating their mortarboards. Approaching their caps as blank canvases, graduates seize this opportunity to make visible individual personality traits, personal experiences, strongly held beliefs, and aesthetic preferences, as well as to display sentiments of appreciation, pride, optimism, relief, uncertainty, or frustration.

While attending another commencement ceremony for UNLV in the spring of 2017, I noticed the decorated mortarboard of a young man sitting in the section of graduates from the College of Liberal Arts. It featured a large image of the face of Donald Trump, who had just taken office as president of the United States a few months before. It also posed the question in big, bold text: "What does my political science degree mean now?" (see figure 1.1). I did not have the opportunity to talk to this graduate about his mortarboard and why he decorated it the way he did, but my initial thoughts were that he was calling attention to the limits of the tools and methods of the discipline of political science to predict the results of the 2016 presidential election. I also speculated that he was lamenting the ways in which this president was, in the words of folklorist Bill Ivey, "ignor[ing] and demean[ing] both democratic customs and their behavioral equivalent: long-established *norms* that establish acceptable, traditional practice in politics and government" (Ivey 2018, 2). In light of this reconfiguration of established norms and traditional practices in the political realm, I understood this graduate to be using his cap to identify a political scene that his college education—one presumably grounded in the scholarly analysis of political activity and behavior—had not equipped him to navigate.

A few months later, I interviewed Christa,[2] another graduate who participated in that same commencement ceremony, and she offered a different interpretation. When I asked her if any of the decorated caps she saw stood out to her, she answered:

> Yes, I think about this one all the time, and it's so funny that you asked me that question. So, there's one that had a picture of Donald Trump, and it said like, "What good is my political science degree now?" or something to that effect. And that killed me because first of all, it was so funny. And second of all, it's accurate, you know? If you have someone who is totally unqualified and is completely stupid, and they're able to just lead the country, no doubt, what good is our education now?

This graduate linked the message of the cap not only to what she perceived as the diminished value of education, but the active valorization and empowerment of explicitly anti-intellectual standpoints embodied by the president at the time.

I cannot be certain what the graduate wearing this decorated mortarboard wanted to communicate by embellishing the cap the way he did, or what audience(s) he was envisioning as he placed it atop his head. I do know, however, that the interpretations this cap inspired, both for me and for his fellow graduate, clearly resonated with broader discourses circulating around higher education in the United States.

Kathleen Manning reminded us over two decades ago that "higher education embraces some suspect purposes within democratic, ostensibly nonelitist American society. These include difficult to visualize, debatable ideals as pursuit of the life of the mind and intellectualism. What does an educated person look like? What is actually gained with a higher education degree? Why should the multiple, often conflicting, purposes of higher education be sanctioned? Why should the public good be invested in this selective system?" (Manning 2000, 46). As a faculty member teaching in the Interdisciplinary Studies program at UNLV, I seek to create space in my classroom for undergraduate students who have chosen a nontraditional major both to reflect on and question how knowledge is structured (or disciplined) in academia, as well as the value and limitations of these structures.[3] And every semester I pay close attention to how students in my classes, many of them first-generation college students, express their views on the purpose and value of pursuing higher education. Conversations with students, both during in-class discussions and outside of class during office hours, have made clear to me that the promises and critiques of higher education—in terms of what it offers, the extent to which it validates or invalidates one's credibility in the workplace and in public discourse—are already part of the discursive landscape of students' everyday lives and therefore are already

Figure 1.1. Decorated mortarboards such as the one on the left are both informed by and responsive to broader discourses about the value of higher education in the United States. Photo credit: Sheila Bock.

informing how students position themselves in relation to their instructors, what they are being taught, and the university as an institution.

Over the course of my research for this book, I have found that decorated mortarboards similarly offer insight into students' thoughtful engagement with the promises and critiques of higher education. In asking the question "What does my political science degree mean now?" on his cap, the graduate pictured above situated himself as someone who had been guided by a belief in the value of the knowledge he gained through a college education only to have it thwarted as he crossed the finish line, a sentiment similarly expressed by Christa's question: "What good is our education now?" Of course, these are not the only frustrations students carry. At a very practical level, many students must take on burdensome amounts of debt to even gain access to what higher education has to offer. Some students enter the college classroom perceiving the university as always already a bastion of left-wing propaganda, positioning their professors from the beginning as antagonists seeking to indoctrinate them.[4] Many others see the university as an institution that was not meant to include them—students of color, students with disabilities, and older students, among others. Discourses of value converge with discourses of belonging, and students see whose voices are (and are not) represented on the syllabus, at the front of the classroom, in the administration of the university—and position themselves accordingly.

University commencement ceremonies function both as rites of passage that mark the transition from student to graduate with an optimistic look toward the future and rites of intensification that affirm the value of higher education. Occupying a "betwixt and between" status in this culturally significant event, many graduates use this symbolically heightened moment to take some control over the meaning of the event (and the accomplishment it represents, the future it envisions) by publicly positioning themselves on their own terms. In the words of one graduate,[5] decorating your cap is "a way to kind of get the final word when you graduate." The widespread practice of decorating mortarboards, one highly visible material genre of reflexive and often ludic expression found in this ritual space, is the subject of this book.

METHODS

After informally observing these caps for several years, both online and during the semiannual UNLV commencement ceremonies that took place each May and December, I began to document the tradition more formally in 2016, photographing decorated caps during commencement ceremonies, interviewing graduates, and putting out calls through social media and via colleagues at different universities for graduates to complete a survey and share images of their decorated mortarboards with me.

While college graduates are not the only ones who decorate their mortarboards—I have seen people participate in the practice at other levels as well, including high school graduations and even graduation-like events marking children's transitions from preschool to kindergarten, or from one elementary-school grade level to another—I have chosen to focus on this population primarily because I am interested in seeing how graduates' participation in this tradition is both informed by and speaking back to prevalent ideas about *higher education* in the United States. A K–12 education is compulsory, but pursuing a college degree is not, though many understand it to be a necessary step to legitimacy and economic security. The college degree is now commonly referred to as "the new high school diploma" as more and more employers are requiring a bachelor's degree at a minimum, though having a bachelor's degree certainly does not guarantee getting one of those jobs. Further, while a person is legally considered an adult at the age of eighteen, popular discourses surrounding the college years often frame it as an important time of transition between adolescence and adulthood, a time of discovering oneself and preparing to embark on the so-called real world. I was interested in exploring the extent to which more widely circulating attitudes about a college education and its value—broadly construed—informed the forms and meanings of the decorated mortarboards worn by college graduates.

From its inception, this project has been informed by folkloristic studies that take performance-centered approaches to material culture (cf. Berlinger 2017; Christensen 2011, 2016, 2017; Shukla 2015). Foregrounding the motivations and interpretations of the individuals who make and use material objects opens up possibilities for understanding the complex, multifaceted beliefs informing people's participation in the practice of wearing embellished graduation caps and the social relationships and broader discursive forces influencing their choices. To these ends, I sought to collect not only examples of decorated mortarboards, but also the interpretations of individuals participating in this tradition through 528 interviews with graduates at UNLV's semiannual commencement ceremonies from 2016 to 2021;[6] forty more-in-depth interviews with graduates from UNLV and other universities; and ninety-six responses to an online survey.[7] Some additional graduates, hearing about my research from others, emailed me individually with written explanations of how and why they decorated their caps the way they did. I conducted the in-depth audio-recorded interviews myself in person or by phone. During UNLV's commencement ceremonies, I worked with student research assistants to interview graduates while they gathered and lined up during the hour before the ceremony began. Most of these interviews were audio-recorded. In cases where they were not, we wrote up field notes about our conversations at the events themselves. The broader call for participation in this research, circulated online via snowball sampling and including the link to the online survey, was crafted to be as inclusive as possible, inviting any college graduate over the age of eighteen who decorated their graduation cap, no matter when they graduated, to take part in the research.

This multipronged approach to documenting individuals' perspectives and motivations yielded responses from individuals graduating between 1991 and 2021, though the majority graduated between 2016 and 2019. Participants ranged in age from twenty-one to seventy-three at the time of their graduation, earning degrees including associate's degrees (AA), bachelor's degrees (BA and BS), and master's degrees (MA, MS, and MSW). They included individuals who identified as women, men, and nonbinary, though the majority identified as women. Self-identified racial and ethnic identities included Arab American, Asian, Asian American, Black, Latina/o/x, Native American, Native Hawaiian, Pacific Islander, and white. Responses came from people who had graduated from different types of institutions of higher education (community colleges, small liberal arts colleges, large universities, religious universities, minority serving institutions, and primarily white institutions) in different regions in the United States. Specific institutions of higher education represented in this study include (in alphabetical order) Boston University; Bowling Green State University; California State University, Northridge; California State University, Sacramento; Central Michigan University; College of Southern Nevada; College of Wooster; Ferris State University; High Point University; Miami University; Michigan State University; Millikin University; Ohio Dominican College; The Ohio State University; Otterbein University; Pittsburgh State University; San Francisco State University; Texas A&M University–Kingsville; Texas Women's University; University of California, Berkeley; University of Denver; University of Houston–Downtown; University of Illinois at Urbana–Champagne; University of Nevada, Las Vegas; University of Nevada, Reno; University of Michigan; Utah State University; and Virginia Tech.

The primary moment of display for these caps during commencement ceremonies is short-lived, but the heightened significance of this ritual event situates the creation, display, and reception of decorated mortarboards within broader social, cultural, and political discourses surrounding higher education in the United States. While seeking out individuals' personal perspectives and motivations for participating in this practice, I also paid close attention to more public framings of this tradition, including how images of mortarboards have grounded online enactments of community through hashtags such as #LetTheFeathersFly and #LatinxGradCaps, as well as what rhetorical framings are employed in news coverage and legal documents in cases where the value of the practice was both called into question and justified.

This project is decidedly qualitative in approach. While I sought to engage with the folk art and perspectives of graduates representing different geographical regions, dates of graduation, and types of institutions, as well as people of different genders, ages, racial and ethnic identities, and areas of study, my primary goal was not to collect representative samples that would allow me to draw conclusions about, for example, which demographics are most likely to include political messages on their caps, how one's group affiliation or geographic location affects the likelihood of decorating one's cap in the first place, or how the key themes visible in the content of these mortarboard displays differ across time, space, and group affiliations. Indeed, the body of materials I collected could not yield adequate answers to these types of questions.[8]

It is also important to highlight here that the materials I collected do not offer a truly comprehensive overview of decorated mortarboards. Not all types of educational institutions are represented, and some demographics are more well-represented than others. Given that I had the opportunity to attend and document this tradition during several ceremonies at my home institution, the majority of people I interviewed graduated with undergraduate degrees from UNLV, a metropolitan research university and primarily commuter campus with roughly thirty thousand students, 30 percent of which are first-generation college students. Ranked among the most diverse undergraduate campuses in the nation by *US News & World Report*, UNLV has been designated a minority-serving institution, Hispanic-serving institution, and Asian American and Native American Pacific Islander–serving institution.

At the same time, though many of the examples introduced throughout this book come from individuals who have graduated from UNLV, these examples have been selected to represent experiences and approaches to decorating mortarboards that are by no means unique to graduates of this specific institution. My approach to data collection and analysis has sought to be inclusive of diverse communities—in terms of race, ethnicity, gender, age, ability, and class-based categories, among others. Through this approach, my aim is to highlight the diverse forms this tradition can take; the multifaceted meanings these crafted objects can carry; and the performative strategies employed as graduates use this creative expressive form to mediate the personal and larger-than-personal, as well as vernacular and institutional perspectives on what higher education has to offer.

PERSONAL ADORNMENT IN A RITUAL CONTEXT

Undoubtedly, dress plays a key role in marking ritual contexts in general and rites of passage in particular. From baptisms to coming-of-age rituals such as first communions and quinceañeras to weddings and funerals, "the individuals who are the focus of these ceremonies tend to dress in a particular way and their attire distinguishes them from the rest of the community" (San Emeterio 2016, 60). Within the ritual space of the commencement ceremony, dress takes on special symbolic meanings as participants don academic dress that has its roots in medieval Europe. Notably, while distinguishing members of the academic community from the rest of the community, this ritual dress marks the differences in status *within* the institutional setting, creating a "hierarchy of robe design" (Bronner 2012, 390). For example, graduates earning a PhD wear a soft velvet tam and a robe with a velvet face running down its front and three velvet stripes on the bell-shaped sleeves. Undergraduates, on the other hand, wear unadorned robes with pointed sleeves and flat, four-sided mortarboards. Dress, then, makes visible the distinctions *between* the educational accomplishments celebrated in the ceremony. The color of graduation robes can also mark distinctions between graduates of different institutions.

While marking these distinctions, the cap and gown typically worn by undergraduates also works to diminish the differences between individuals in a graduating class. In other words, the ritual function of dress during commencement foregrounds what graduates have in common—their transitional status and their role within the university—over what makes them unique. Often, universities will provide graduates with honor cords to mark their field of study or academic achievements. While these colorful cords do visually mark distinctions between graduates, they still work to align graduates with group affiliations and values sanctioned by the university as a whole.

The practice of decorating mortarboards is one manifestation of a broader practice of adapting the ritual dress of the commencement ceremony, one that is certainly not new. In her book *Clothing Concepts*, Mary Lou Rosencranz describes how,

> during the period of student unrest and student strikes in the spring of 1970, some graduation exercises were performed under unusual circumstances and in unusual costume. Academic robes were changed by the addition of new symbols. Tradition was shattered by placing peace signs on mortarboards; peace doves, clenched fists, or flags on the backs of robes; the wearing of hippie jewelry over the robes, white armbands on the arms, and the foreswearing of caps and gowns altogether at some institutions. (Rosencranz 1972, 300)

In their study of the personalization of graduation attire at a large Western university during 1982 and 1983, psychologists identified a range of examples, including instances of political forms of adornment, specifically green ribbons distributed by peace activists, and nonpolitical forms of adornment, including buttons, balloons, flowers, flags, signs, masks, and automobile license plates (Harrison et al. 1986).

The adaptation of ritual dress can take different forms, including opting *not* to wear the cap and gown at all, often replacing this symbolic dress with adornment the graduate finds to be more personally meaningful. A friend and colleague of mine, for example, explained how in 1994, she and a fellow women's studies major chose not to wear graduation gowns, donning instead "regular" clothes and sashes bearing statistics about contemporary women's issues in order to bring attention to the problems of domestic violence and unequal pay.

In 2015, one Native Hawaiian graduate of the University of Hawai'i Hawai'inuiākea donned his malo, a traditional Hawaiian loincloth, to participate in a traditional chant, or oli, at the beginning of the ceremony with a group of fellow students. He put his graduation gown on over his malo after the oli was complete, expecting to wear the gown for the duration of the ceremony, though he later changed his mind and decided he wanted to show his cultural pride by standing on the stage and receiving his diploma while wearing only the malo. He later explained: "Whether you are Hawaiian, Maori, Samoan, Tongan, or whatever culture you claim . . . know your roots, represent, and perpetuate. Not just for yourself, but for your family, your ancestors, and the future generations of your culture" (Wang 2015).

The practice of wearing kente stoles, brightly colored scarves made from red, green, blue, and gold kente cloth, became a common part of commencement ceremonies at historically black institutions in the mid-1980s, and it began to increase in visibility in primarily white institutions in the early 1990s. According to a 1995 article in *The Chronicle of Higher Education*, "Students say the stoles, decorated with patterns once favored by African royalty, show solidarity among black classmates and honor their heritage" (Gose 1995). Other historically marginalized groups have adopted similar traditions, such as Latina/o/x graduates donning serape scarves.

In Hawaii, the traditional practice of giving leis infuses the visual landscape of the ceremony. The graduation tradition of wearing leis of different materials (including flowers, money, and candy) is visible in many commencement ceremonies all over the country, practiced by both transplanted Hawaiians and non-Hawaiians—though for many it is intertwined with broader cultural belief systems. In a 1999 *New York Times* article, celebrated lei maker Barbara Meheula explained how "parents will hike in a storm to gather maile [a culturally significant native plant] for their child's graduation, because it signifies that the child will continue to grow and have life. . . . Maile represents life and growth" (Fujii 1999). Indigenous people who live in other parts of the United States similarly integrate cultural beliefs and practices into the ritual space of commencement ceremonies, for example by attaching an eagle feather to their mortarboard or by embellishing their cap with traditional beading.

To be clear, self-consciously adapting the official regalia (or opting not to wear it) is not the only way graduates use their dress on commencement day as a mode of self-expression. The conventional cap and gown are, after all, only part of the graduates' creative assemblage of bodily adornment.[9] Dress is a rich communicative resource individuals use to position themselves in relation to different social categories, including gender, race, ethnicity, socioeconomic status, age, nationality, region, and religion. The bodily adornment that is visible during the ceremony (hair, makeup, jewelry, nail art, tattoos, shoes, material of pants or skirts that fall under the knee) cue to others this social positioning, and even the bodily adornment that is *not* visible under the gown is selected with intention, and thus carries meaning. The various choices made at the level of dress, independently of the ritual dress of the cap and gown, is shaped by "the individual's personality, style history, social identifications, finances, interpersonal relationships, and sense of place" (Hertz 2013, 381).

AT THE INTERSECTIONS OF THE PERSONAL AND THE TRADITIONAL

This book is grounded in my training in folklore studies, a field attentive to vernacular beliefs and practices, the dynamics of tradition, and the aesthetic modes people use to create and communicate meaning in their lives. Viewing decorated mortarboards through this lens, I was drawn from the beginning to the artistry and creativity of many of these material displays. I recognized how each mortarboard display claimed the blank space of the mortarboard, reconfiguring the ritual dress into traditional performances of the personal. Building on this recognition, I wanted to understand how the (textual, visual, material) messages on the caps both aligned with and diverged from the institutional messaging structuring the commencement event as a whole.

In addition to noting practical considerations such as wanting to be visible to friends and family members in the audience, many of the people I interviewed for this project referenced the desire for *personal* expression in the space of the commencement ceremony as a key motivation for participating. For example:

"I wanted to express myself as I am."

"I wanted to pick something that represented me."

"[Decorating your cap] gives you a chance to be unique and show your personality. It's a way to express yourself."

"The cap is a way to put yourself into the graduation since it is *your* personal achievement. It's a way to give it your personal touch."

Popular understandings of the practice of decorating mortarboards similarly focus on how they function as sites of personal expression. A 2019 feature on decorated mortarboards in the *New York Times*, for example, was titled "Wearing Their Hearts on Their Graduation Caps." Adapting the popular saying "wear one's heart on one's sleeve," which is used in situations where someone makes their personal feelings and sentiments visible to others, this headline situates the practice as one where the personal is put on display for public audiences.

In addition to being sites of personal expression, decorated mortarboards are undoubtedly traditional. As noted by Alan Dundes and Carl Pagter, the label "traditional" can be applied to expressive forms when "they manifest multiple existence in space and time, and they exist in variant forms" (Dundes and Pagter [1978] 1992, xvii). The practice of decorating mortarboards clearly illustrates these key characteristics of multiple existence and variation, not only in the act of decorating (which is both widespread geographically in the United States and recurring year after year) but also in the content of the displays. To take just one example, consider the prevalence of one classic message found on these caps—"Thanks Mom and Dad"—and the adaptations that emerge such as "thank you Starbucks and Dad's Gold Card," "thanks Mom and Uncle Sam," and "thank you Google." The established nature of decorating mortarboards as a traditional form of folk expression is further evidenced by the metafolkloric nature of some designs, which offer folk commentary on the nature of the genre as a whole (Dundes 1966). One graduate, for example, wore a cap adorned with the words, "[insert inspirational quote HERE]," making a reference to a common feature of many decorated caps (see figure 1.2).

The content of many caps includes other genres of traditional folk speech, including proverbs (e.g., "a smooth sea never made a skillful sailor," "out of the frying pan and into the fire," "never trust a skinny chef") and wordplay. The cap of one math major I interviewed, for example, included the phrase "life just got real," creating an inside joke for people who understood the reference to real numbers in mathematics. Another graduate, a computer science major, put "C++ get degrees" on his cap, transforming the popular folk saying "C's get degrees" with a reference to the programming language C++. The mortarboard of Amber, a chemistry major, included the words "keep calm and Curie on," an adaptation of the phrase "keep calm and carry on" found on posters created by the British government during World War II. During our 2016 interview, Amber explained: "I grew up learning about Marie Curie. She was a huge influence on my

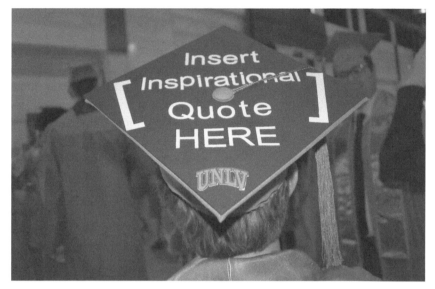

Figure 1.2. Decorated mortarboards have become such an established expressive genre that common generic features are playfully referenced in the designs themselves. Photo credit: Sheila Bock.

decision to pursue a chemistry degree. I loved the history of the discovery and isolation of certain radioactive elements and just wanted to pay tribute to her." She also saw this phrase as a reference to the research she did on radioactive elements while pursuing her degree, as well as the pride she felt from being a woman in science.

Other caps reference particular genres of folk expression, such as one first-generation college student who wrote "no blonde joke" on the top of her cap in 1992. "Blonde jokes were popular at the time," she explained in her survey response, "and this was a statement about being taken seriously as a blonde female. People liked to tell me blonde jokes because my hair was very blonde. I usually thought they were funny and appreciated the humor. My mortarboard was a way of responding back that I wasn't the stereotypical dumb blonde girl from the jokes. I graduated magna cum laude and Phi Beta Kappa so I had the 'creds' to back it up."

Many caps also share themes with other documented forms of humor surrounding graduation in general, including "satirical readings of collegiate initialism" (Bronner 2012, 403) through phrases such as "finally done with this B.S." (playing on the double meaning of BS as standing for "bachelor of science" and "bullshit"). Others draw on humor mocking particular occupation groups, such as one cap worn by an engineering graduate mocking the anti-intellectualism of engineers also found in Xeroxlore documented by Dundes and Pagter (1987, 212–214). It reads: "I'm an ENGENEER ENGINERE ENGENERE I'm good at math."

While initially the notion of the "traditional" might seem at odds with the "personal," folkloristic scholarship has shown how expressive acts that are marked or understood as personal are in fact always larger than personal. That is, expressions of the personal are always social and relational. The genre of personal experience narratives has received the most attention in this regard. In her groundbreaking work on this genre, for example, Sandra Stahl (Dolby) (1977, 1989) showed that while on the surface stories within this genre appear idiosyncratic, they are informed by and reflective of culturally shared values and attitudes that are, in fact, traditional. Kate Parker Horigan (2018) further considers the larger-than-personal dynamics at play when narrative recountings of personal experience meet public audiences that are not familiar with the narrator, especially in light of the inherently social nature of the creation, transmission, and function of personal narratives.

Performing the personal in public can be a risky endeavor, as performers can lose control over how the story should be interpreted once it is out in the world and open to recontextualization (Shuman 2005). Scholars such as Horigan (2018) and Willsey (2015) have recognized how performers of personal narratives have a heightened awareness of shifting modes of evaluation due to larger political discourses, culturally informed narrative conventions, and social expectations. In light of these shifting contexts of evaluation, narrators often craft their stories in ways that allow them to retain some control over the interpretation of their experiences. Engaging with similar issues in her study of scrapbooks, a material culture genre that, like the genre of mortarboard displays, is simultaneously marked as personal and meant for display, Danille Christensen (2016) identifies material and other performative strategies of negotiation embedded in the objects themselves and how their creators choose to present them to others.

Recognizing that such genres of expressive culture become sites where the relationships between the personal and the public are mediated, this book explicitly considers how decorated mortarboards occupy the different categories of "personal" and "larger than personal." In the process, it shows how these performances of the personal take shape in relation to broader, ongoing conversations about higher education in the United States, conversations grounded in discourses of belonging, citizenship, and the promises of the American dream.

DIALOGIC ACTS OF POSITIONING AND
PERFORMING SOCIAL SELVES

In approaching mortarboard displays as traditional performances of the personal, I also understand them as dialogic acts of positioning. By *dialogic*, I am drawing on the work on Mikhail Bakhtin, specifically the idea that the meanings of creative expressions—indeed, all acts of expression—are both carried over from the past and emergent in the present. Recognizing the dialogic nature of all expressive acts, we understand that references to previous discourses are not just referential, they can be generative and transformational.

A cap worn by Ari, a graduate who had transitioned from female to male during his time as a university student, included text that read "college made me a man" against the background of the trans flag.[10] As he explained in our 2019 interview, "you kind of associate 'made me a man' with hyper-masculinity . . . like 'I went to the military and it really made me a man,' or coming of age, but also the toughening of it. And I sort of felt like I was subverting that and connecting it directly with my queerness." Through the design of this cap, the commonly used meaning of the phrase transformed to adapt to the graduate's life experiences, enacting alternate visions of what it means to be made a man.

Discursive references do not have to be textual—they can be material and visual as well. One graduate, using the hashtag #LatinxGradCaps, posted an image of a cap online that incorporated fabric from a piece of clothing that belonged to her grandmother. The accompanying caption read:

> As I wrapped my grandmother's work dress around my cap I could not help but feel overwhelmed with tears as I channeled her strength to be where I am today. I could not have done it without her, my mother or my daughters. "Here's to strong women, may we know them. May we be them. May we raise them."[11]

This material reference integrated clothing associated with physical labor into the ritual dress associated with academic success. In the process, it marked her grandmother's story as part of her own, situating the accomplishment of attaining a college degree as not just an *individual* accomplishment but as part of an ongoing *family* story characterized by hard work and strength.

Other mortarboards feature the gesture of a raised fist (sometimes holding up a diploma), indexing meanings of resistance and solidarity, particularly in contexts of racial oppression (see figures 1.3 and 1.4).

Figure 1.3. Through their language and imagery, caps can be transformed into overt sites of political expression. Photo credit: Sheila Bock.

Figure 1.4. Decorated mortarboards can work to position the graduate in relation to broader identity categories. Photo credit: Nicole Cristina Espinosa.

Accompanied by phrases such as "By Any Means Necessary" (a slogan popularized by Black civil rights activist Malcolm X in 1964), "beware bad hombre with degree" (referencing presidential candidate Donald Trump's characterization of Mexican men crossing the southern US-Mexican border as "bad hombres"), and "you cannot oppress the people who are not afraid anymore!" (a quote from Mexican American labor organizer and civil rights activist Cesar Chavez), these gestural references transform these moments of individual celebration into overt acts of political expression, framing the very act of completing the college degree as an act of resistance.

In approaching mortarboard displays as acts of *positioning*, I am drawing on multiple strands of scholarship. Folklorist Pravina Shukla (2005) has shown how personal adornment choices serve as modes of social positioning that mark, among other things, social standings, relationships, and affiliations. As she explains, "One of the main functions fulfilled by dress is to mark the multiple identities of individuals, and therefore, to position them within their social networks" (2005).[12] Analyzing different types of material, specifically the interactional contexts of storytelling, narrative scholars have similarly looked at the ways individuals position themselves and how positions are "locally occasioned and designed, they are temporally and situationally flexible, and they are multifaceted—that is, different facets of identity are relevant in different contexts" (Deppermann 2015, 370). Narrative scholars have used the concept of positioning to consider how individuals situate themselves not only in relation to social contexts but also in relation to master narratives (Bamberg and Georgakopoulou 2008) and identity categories (Slocum-Bradley 2009). Bringing the insights of these different strands of scholarship together to frame my analysis of mortarboard displays helps illuminate the ways in which they work to situate the individuals who wear them in relation to broader contexts that ground the individual as a social actor, contexts that influence how individuals choose to craft these material acts of self-expression.

For example, one recurring pattern I have observed in many caps is the way individuals use them to perform relational or social selves; that is, to position themselves in term of their relationships and affiliations with others (see figure 1.5). Sometimes these relationships can be marked when two or more people coordinate their plans for adorning their caps. A group of six friends and classmates, for example, made a spontaneous decision while attending a college reception before the larger university commencement to take the red balloons adorning the reception hall and to affix them to their caps. In another instance, a couple coordinated their caps so that both featured imagery from the Pixar movie *Finding Nemo*. Twin sisters also coordinated their caps with imagery from *Finding Nemo*. "Do you have your exit buddy?" one read. "Yes, I have my exit buddy," said the other. As one of this pair explained, "I wanted to make graduation specifically with my sister more memorable."

Figure 1.5. Individuals often decorate mortarboards in ways that visibly mark important relationships in their lives. Photo credit: Sheila Bock.

Coordinated caps are not just used to mark human relationships. During one commencement ceremony at The Ohio State University, a graduate gave his service dog a small mortarboard to wear (see figure 1.6). "OH," the dog's cap proclaimed in bold, red letters, while the graduate's cap read, "IO." Together, these caps referenced the cheer commonly used by Ohio State football fans, a cheer set up as a type of call and response. One or more people will shout "O-H!" (at a football game or even out in the city of Columbus), and the response will come: "I-O!" As a cheer, it marks the people who participate in it as part of a clear Ohio State community, even if they do not know each other. Recontextualized into the visual space of these caps at a commencement ceremony, this chant not only positions both the graduate and his dog as part of the larger Ohio State community, it also marks the service dog as a significant part of the graduate's college experience.[13]

Relationships can also be marked in the *process* of decorating one's mortarboard. I have interviewed several graduates who chose to decorate their cap in the first place because a friend or a classmate organized a gathering for that purpose, so that sociability motivates their participation in the tradition. These events typically take place immediately following final exams, so they very often function as a kind of "stress break," in the words of one of my interviewees, a way to relax and take a break from responsibilities. They also function as moments of reflection. Graduate Briceida explained:

Figure 1.6. Decorated mortarboards can mark meaningful human–animal relationships. Photo credit: Cassie Rosita Patterson for the Folklore Archives for the Center for Folklore Studies at The Ohio State University [GCT(OSU)20171217CP83].

Decorating [my cap] with friends was a way I could reminisce about our journeys into and through college, while also celebrating our accomplishments together. In fact, I actually created an event where I and fellow graduating Latinx students could get together over food to decorate our caps in preparation for the upcoming Latinx graduation celebration. . . . I cherished the time spent with friends being silly and working on my cap. I think during these stressful moments in one's life, when you're thinking of the future, it's nice to have time for fun, creativity, and community.

For many, the process of decorating the mortarboard is a collaborative one. One year, for example, when UNLV's commencement was the day before Mother's Day, a graduate worked with his younger sister to craft his cap so that it said "Happy Mother's Day Mom UNLV 2017." When asked why he selected this message, he explained that his mom was one of the most important people in his life, and he thought it would make a good Mother's Day gift for her—one both he and his sister made together.[14] Another graduate that same year, a woman from Germany who came to the United States to play collegiate volleyball, had a cap that proclaimed "herzliche glückwünsche Elli," which translates from German to "Congratulations Elli." The cap was adorned by gold wrappers from chocolates brought by her family from Germany that were craftily repurposed into the shape of flowers. During an interview, she explained that even though this is not a tradition in her home country of Germany, her mother and grandmother decorated the cap after flying from Germany to Las Vegas to attend UNLV's commencement. While she had the basic idea for the design, her family members executed it. The content of the display, both textually and materially, indexed the graduate's German origins and her familial relationships. Yet another UNLV graduate integrated a haku lei into her cap, explaining that she is from Hawaii, and she wanted something to commemorate her home state. Her cousin had provided the materials by bringing the haku lei from Hawaii.

Some of the graduates I interviewed about their caps explained how they did not participate at all in the process of decorating their mortarboards. In some cases, others took charge of the process upon hearing that the graduate was not sufficiently motivated or inspired to decorate it themselves.[15] In other cases, loved ones surprised them with decorated mortarboards, presenting them as gifts.[16] One graduate, for example, was surprised by her mom and aunt, who decorated her cap when they realized she would not have time to do it herself. Knowing that that she loved the music of J. Cole, a rapper that she listened to while she studied, they put one of his lyrics on her mortarboard: "life is your professor, know that bitch is gonna test ya."

The content of these mortarboard displays was often imbued with the significance of family relationships, even when family members did not participate in the decorating process, as in the case of one graduate whose cap featured images of bumblebees in reference to the nickname her parents gave her when she was a small child. Another graduate's cap featured the text, "I have done a smart thing." When I asked her why she put those words on her cap, she replied, "Growing up my parents always had their respective sayings they would send us off to school with, and my dad's was 'Do smart things.' And so I took that and I turned it around as a kind of honor to him to say 'I have done a smart thing.'" Another graduate's cap featured a fake lau lau (a traditional Hawaiian dish) made of cotton balls and ribbon and the words "graduating Summa Cum Lau-Lau." Honoring her great-aunt, who played a large role in her family moving to America from the Philippines (as well as her love of Hawaiian food), the way she decorated her cap also referenced a joke her mom cracked about graduation that she found hilarious. As she explained in her survey response, "It's nice to bring something tied to my family with me as I walk onto that stage." Yet another graduate decorated her cap with large, glittery letters that read "Live your story. Faith, hope, glory," referencing the theme song to the 1988 children's movie *The Land Before Time* sung by Diana Ross, called "If We Hold on Together." Her mom, she said, has an old home movie of the graduate and her sister when they were children. In the home movie, she is singing that song to her mother, so the song has always been important to the three of them. Her cap also included an old black-and-white photograph of her grandparents, who had passed away the year before.

I observed many caps that similarly served as memorials for important people in graduates' lives who had passed away. One graduate whose cap featured a photograph of her grandmother, who was very supportive of her in school, explained: "That way she is walking with me." She decorated the cap with her mom, making the process, in her words, "kind of a Mother's Day thing." Another cap included a photo of the graduate as a child with her dad. She explained that her dad passed away four years earlier after being in a coma for several years due to a car accident. She wanted to honor him because he was always a great proponent of education, even though he never finished high school himself. Many of the mortarboard displays I documented also positioned graduates in terms of religious beliefs and affiliations, for example through references to Bible verses and Gospel lyrics.

While it is common for graduates to highlight affiliations with the university, their major, and student organizations, it is equally common in my observations for graduates to highlight relationships that extend beyond the university community. In many cases, I observed mortarboard displays that highlighted both. In one example, a graduate, Claudia, decorated their cap with a vibrant, glittery background and the presentation of two phrases, "viaja aprende sirve" and "K byeee." The first phrase referenced Alternative Breaks, an organization on campus that played a big part in their college experience:

> Their tagline is "Learn, Travel, Serve" because we travel to nearby cities, and do service work *with* the local community, while also learning about the social justice issues involved. I've learned so much about the world, myself, and leadership through this. I've led trips to San Diego focused on immigration, and Carson City focused on indigenous issues, and both trips had a huge impact on me.

Being a native speaker of Spanish, this was also something Claudia wished to highlight on their cap: "I wrote 'Learn, Travel, Serve' in Spanish because it was one way to communicate that the language is mine, and these identities go together." The second phrase, "K byeee!" is a catchphrase from *My Favorite Murder*, a popular, funny true-crime podcast. Including it in their cap not only served as a way to bid farewell to being an undergraduate student, it marked them as a "murderino," an active participant in this larger (non-academic) fandom community.[17]

The diverse range of group affiliations and relationships indexed in both the mortarboard displays and the processes by which they are decorated should not be surprising, especially if we consider cultural anthropologist Rebekah Nathan's assertion that "there is little that is automatically shared among people by virtue of attending the same university" (Nathan 2006, 39). Thus, students' experiences of "community" while pursuing a degree form just as much (if not more) around personal networks and everyday experiences as institutional affiliations. Graduates, then, often use the process of decorating their caps to reflect on—and in many cases bring attention to—the importance of these communities and relationships not otherwise visible within the more formal structures of the commencement ritual.

The role of "student" is just one aspect of people's identities as they make their way through higher education, even for those who reach the institutionally recognized benchmarks of academic success, such as high GPAs. For the most part, other aspects of identity and one's sense of self—such as family roles and responsibilities or even sense of humor—are not inherently valued in the academic arena, and often are seen as standing in the way of student success in the classroom. Furthermore, bigger universities have become notorious for frustrating bureaucracies that fail to take into account the needs and desires of individuals. As one professor at a large state school quipped, "At [name of university], some students think they are just a number, but that's not true. Here, you are not even a number. You are a barcode." Situating his own study of decorated graduation caps, specifically among graduates of color, within a context of neoliberal restructuring in higher education, sociologist Esa Syeed considers how "these caps may serve as a way to reclaim their personhood in alienating spaces" (Syeed 2020, 366).

The formalized structure of the commencement ceremony diminishes personal differences, ritually dramatizing much of students' experiences within their institution. As discussed earlier, the ritual dress of commencement is a significant way that graduates' individuality is symbolically erased

Figure 1.7. Graduates often use the space of the mortarboard to highlight aspects of their identity and experiences that extend beyond their role as a student. Photo credit: Sheila Bock.

within the formalized ritual space of commencement, though it is certainly not the only one. As Simon Bronner explains, at many large institutions, graduates "are recognized simply by quickly standing together in the midst of a huge arena" (Bronner 2012, 393). Even when they get to walk across the stage, their moment in the spotlight is brief, and often their individual names might not even be called. Graduates who *are* highlighted as award recipients or student speakers are most often selected because of their academic success, and they are introduced as embodying the core university values being performed within the commencement ritual. Individual identities are invoked to affirm their membership in, and solidarity with, the university community more broadly. Put on display in this broader institutional context, the blank canvas of the mortarboard provides students the opportunity to claim some of this ritual space and make visible those nonacademic aspects of themselves that they wish to be publicly represented. Consider the cap of one graduate, adorned with United States flags, toy soldiers, and the seal of the United States Army, along with the words: "one shot one kill thank you GI Bill" (see figure 1.7). Referencing the occupational folk speech of the sniper team he led while serving in the military, service that included a thirteen-month deployment in Iraq, this cap served as a way of marking—and valuing—this part of his life.

Figure 1.8. Sometimes elements of the mortarboard's design are selected with the intention of offering implicit critiques of the university setting. Photo credit: Nicole Cristina Espinosa.

In the interview data collected for this study, the claiming of this ritual space is not always presented as an intentional critique of the way individuals are positioned within the university setting, but sometimes it is, as we see in the explanation offered by one graduate about the different elements she incorporated into her cap's design (see figure 1.8):

> I chose pink because it reflects my femininity, especially in this space which makes you kind of be asexualized because it is considered to be inappropriate. So I chose pink. I highlighted the word "ho" in "Scholar" because that is the source of my scholarship [as a gender and sexuality studies major] and my identity and my personality within this space. And I also chose a cactus sticker because it commemorates resistance, especially in this non-forgiving climate that we call academia.

As many of the mortarboard displays are shaped by how individuals are positioned by the university as institution, they are also informed by discourses surrounding higher education, and they position individuals in relation to these broader discourses. While there are certainly multiple discourses framing prevalent understandings of higher education in the

United States (e.g., college is a space and time of transition from adolescence to adulthood; college is a time of self-discovery; college is the time of one's life), one particularly powerful and enduring narrative is that pursuing higher education is a key stepping stone in achieving the American dream, a narrative grounded in the "American folk idea of college paving the way to commercial success" (Bronner 2012, 9).

The popularization of the phrase "American dream" can be traced back to author James Truslow Adams's 1931 book *The Epic of America*. According to Adams, the American dream is one "of social order in which each man and each woman shall be able to attain to the fullest stature of which they are innately capable, and be recognized by others for what they are, regardless of the fortuitous circumstances of birth or position" (1931, 404). This idea has been a prevalent force in the history of the United States. Some of the core values that have consistently shaped the idea of the American dream in both the past and the present include freedom, equality of opportunity, and individual rights, along with hard work, perseverance, and an enduring optimism for eventual success (Cullen 2003; Terkel 1980; White 2016).

Decorated caps often align individuals with this widely circulating narrative (for example, with phrases like "better things to come" and "my future is unlimited"), but they can also complicate them, as in the case of the cap introduced at the beginning of this introduction, and as will become apparent in the following chapters. Taking mortarboard displays seriously as traditional performances of the personal and dialogic acts of positioning, this book highlights the creative, playful, and powerful ways graduates use their caps to fashion (quite literally) their personal engagement with notions of self, education, community, and the unknown future.

CHAPTER OUTLINE AND A NOTE ON AUDIENCE

Chapter 2 expands upon some of the key ideas presented in the introduction through a more in-depth consideration of these mortarboard displays as sites of performance. Drawing heavily on the voices and perspectives of graduates thoughtfully reflecting on their participation in this tradition, this chapter illuminates how multifaceted notions of self are envisioned, enacted, and negotiated; the dialogic nature of these processes; and how these performances of self are positioned in relation to the dominant discourses structuring experiences of belonging and exclusion in spaces of higher education.

Given that the commencement ceremony is the primary context of display and interpretive frame for decorated mortarboards, chapter 3 brings focused attention to this ritual context and the visual, embodied rhetorics of belonging embedded within it. The cap and gown play a key role in the function of the ceremony as a "show of community" (Bronner 2012, 388) marked by unity, uniformity, and formality. This chapter identifies how exclusions are enacted in these visual performances of community, both explicitly and implicitly, and the tangible ways graduates respond to these exclusions.

Chapter 4 moves beyond the commencement ceremony as the primary site of performance and examines how social media platforms provide opportunities for new contexts of display that engage with different and more widespread audiences. Looking specifically at images and stories posted online with the popular #LatinxGradCaps hashtag, it addresses how the aesthetic and narrative framings of Latinx identities in these online displays individually and collectively work to disrupt and reframe *both* prevalent cultural narratives about Latinx communities in the United States *and* how discourses of citizenship converge with popular interpretations of the American dream.

Chapter 5 further considers how decorated mortarboards engage with the promises embedded in the American dream. Specifically, it argues that we can understand the ambivalence and inversions we often see on display on these caps to be transforming them into sites of rearticulation, expressive sites that engage in the work of *un*disciplining not only in the space of commencement, but also the broader cultural narratives about success that shape it. Finally, the conclusion offers reflections on how I see this book engaging in the work of countertrivialization (Fivecoate, Downs, and McGriff 2021) and identifies potential pathways of inquiry that build upon and extend the insights offered in this text.

Before bringing this introductory chapter to a close, I have one more note on the audience for this book. It is my hope that the ideas shared in the following pages will be of interest to other scholars, both within and outside my home discipline of folklore studies. It is equally important to me that I communicate these ideas in a way that is accessible to students who may be thinking about these topics for the first time. The insights I have gained into the complex dynamics shaping this material genre of expressive culture are indebted to the people (primarily recent undergraduates) who shared their experiences with and interpretations of this tradition with me. My goal, then, has been to write a book that undergraduate students who are relatively new to the study of traditional expressive culture could not only learn from but also enter into conversation with. Ultimately, I hope this book opens up spaces (both inside and outside the classroom) to continue valuing and engaging with students' perspectives, experiences, and modes of self-presentation.

2

Crafting Performances of Self

SELF-CONSCIOUS PUBLIC DISPLAYS THAT are set apart from everyday communication, decorated mortarboards constitute a material genre of performance. While different performance genres function differently, according to Deborah Kapchan, "all actively create social and individual identities in the public domain" (Kapchan 2003, 130). In this chapter, I approach the caps as crafted material objects, and I seek to highlight how graduates engage in performances of self through these material displays, performances of self that are shaped by different (though often overlapping) social and discursive forces. Interspersed throughout this chapter is a sampling of vignettes featuring ten different graduates and the graduation caps they wore, foregrounding their voices as they shared with me some of the decision-making processes that informed how and why they decorated their mortarboards. Both individually and as a group, how these graduates talk about their decorated caps offers insight into the multifaceted performances these material forms of expressive culture engender. Representing a range of motivations and approaches to personalizing their mortarboards, these vignettes also illustrate some recurring modes of performance apparent in this material tradition more broadly—particularly as they relate to performing the personal and mediating how the meanings embedded in these crafted performances are communicated to and negotiated for different audiences. Ultimately, this chapter illuminates how multifaceted notions of self are envisioned, enacted, and negotiated; the dialogic nature of these processes; and how these performances of self that are put on display through this material genre are positioned in relation to dominant discourses structuring experiences of belonging and exclusion in spaces of higher education.

 https://doi.org/10.7330/9781646425259.c002

VIGNETTE #1

When Brenda graduated with her bachelor's degree in 2017, the design of her cap included the quote: "vuela tan alto como puedas sin olvidar de donde vienes," which translates from Spanish to "fly as high as you can without forgetting where you come from." She explained in our 2018 interview her reasoning for including these words:

> It was finally coming to the end of undergrad, like coming to this point in my life, and looking back at everything that not only *I* had done but everything that *my family* had done and everything that my *community* has done, and every way that we have grown. And kind of remembering why we do the things that we do. You know, like, we can grow as much as possible as individuals, as families, as communities. We can grow as much as possible, but we always have to remember where we come from, where our roots are from, why it is that we do the things we do.

I asked her why she does the things that she does, and she responded:

> I am undocumented. I've lived basically my whole life since I was two in Las Vegas. I've gone to school here, and right after high school I really contemplated the idea of going back to Mexico, because I graduated in 2012. . . . And back then, I had told not a living soul that I was undocumented. I think only my family knew, and maybe like one or two friends knew, but we didn't know the extent, or I didn't know the extent of what that meant. . . . I think it was a month after I graduated that President Barack Obama announced DACA [Deferred Action for Childhood Arrivals], announced this relief for undocumented children that had come at such a young age, and were studying, were trying to go to school, get jobs, and really be a part of the only country that we've known. So that came into my life at a point where I really was contemplating, like I had no future here. I can't do much here, so it might just be best for me to go back. And so, when DACA came out, my family found every way possible to try and pay for the application. And after that, that's when I kind of started getting involved with my community, and helping other students and helping other families, you know, understand DACA and get paperwork ready, and that's pretty much where I guess I got my roots of being an activist. It was having the opportunity to give back to my community. Like, putting my application in, there was this adrenaline in me that said like, now you have to go out and do it for other people.

Brenda first earned her associate's degree at a local community college, graduating with a cap emblazoned with the words "undocugrad and proud." As she planned her cap for her graduation for her bachelor's degree in 2017, she considered featuring a similar message—"Undocumented, Unafraid, Unapologetic"—though she ultimately chose not to:[1]

> I realized that when I graduated before [prior to the election of Donald Trump], we were under a completely different kind of presidential rhetoric than we are now [in the year 2018]. And it wasn't so much a fear of having someone say something to me or anything like that. It was just more of having that day be special and not having to worry about the stigmas that are out there for undocumented students. So I just wanted it to be a special day to celebrate everything that had been done throughout the years to get to this point.

Brenda thought primarily about her family when she chose to display the quote in Spanish, though she had other audiences in mind as well: "As long as [my family has] been here and they understand the language, and they have become accustomed to being in America and everything, [Spanish] is the first language that I learned. It's the first language that they know. And I think putting it in Spanish also puts that idea that, yes, I am Hispanic and I am proud of that. And I am proud of where I come from, and being able to communicate in a completely other language."

Brenda also adorned her cap with images of butterflies, symbols of immigrant rights activism, as well as real flowers, flowers that carried specific meanings. "There are different kinds of marigolds," she explained, "but one of them, in Latino culture, it's the *cempasúchil*, which is the flower of the dead. And during that [Día de Muertos] celebration, when people pass, that's the flower they use. And so recently, this past year, while I was doing my last year of undergrad, my grandpa passed away. And the last time that I had seen him was I think when I was 8 or 9, because he then left back to Mexico, and the only way that we had contact or anything was through phone calls. So, it just, I felt like I had to find a way to represent him in everything that I was doing and honor him as well."

After she finished decorating her cap, Brenda put it next to a photograph of her grandfather on display in her family's living room, and she took a picture. "I didn't post that one on social media," she told me. "That was more for myself to keep."

VIGNETTE #2

According to Ronna, the theme of her cap was "it's never too late." This was actually the text she put on her cap, along with "'73" on the left-hand side, indicating the year she graduated high school (1973), and "'14" on the right-hand side, indicating the year she graduated from college (2014). The "'73" was purple, since her high school's colors were purple and white. The "'14" was red, to represent her college colors. She wanted something else on there, so she decided to reference a side hobby she actively participates in: showing purebred cats.

"So, my cattery is called 'Dreamers,'" Ronna told me in 2018, "and my daughter was pretty much raised in the cat fancy, and she has her own cattery that she calls 'Believers.' So that's why I put 'DREAM' on the top, and then on the bottom, it says 'BELIEVE.' It's to remind people to believe in your dreams and never stop, and that it's never too late."

That message is communicated to people who don't know her personally and to people who know her well. The ideas of "dreaming" and "believing," though added later in her decorating process to help fill in some of the empty space, were very central to the message she wanted to communicate:

> I wanted to make sure I incorporated dreaming and believing because
> it had always been a dream of mine to someday—well, when I was
> in high school, things were different in 1973. I would have gone
> to Northwestern. I grew up in Chicago, and I would have gone to
> Northwestern and majored in Journalism. Well, things were different,
> and I spent four years in high school just wanting to get out. . . . Years
> later, I regretted that I made the choices I made in high school. And I
> regretted that I never got a degree, and I always wanted to. And I ended
> up at Ohio State when [the school district I worked for] was making cut-
> backs and I was let go.

The first time Ronna tried to decorate her cap, it didn't turn out as she had planned and she had to redo it: "So then I was like, okay, so now how can I cover up what I've done? And that's when I thought I would take a section of *The Lantern* [the school newspaper]. And it was a section of paper that had pictures that I had taken for one of my classes, and I got a photo credit for it. So I thought, okay, well, that will cover up the mistake. . . . It was a moment of desperation."

Despite this change in her initial plan, she was pleased with how it turned out: "I was very happy with the end result because it was exactly representing me, and it was exactly what I wanted to say. And the newspaper was just an added bonus . . . so it kind of came out of a mess, but I liked it very much. And it was definitely me."

After the graduation ceremony, she thought: "Now what do I do with it?" So, she decided to put it up on her wall at work. "It hangs on my cubicle wall to remind me, don't stop dreaming, don't stop believing. And now, I'm back in school. I will be 63 going back to grad school." She further described this new context of display for her decorated cap:

> My cubicle at work is very reflective of my personality and who I am. I have a collection of cats that I have on a shelf. My husband travels overseas a lot. He's a CFA [Cat Fanciers' Association] judge and judges at the cat shows. So, he'll bring back little ceramic cats for me, so I have a bookshelf of cats. I have frames with my family members, and then on one of my overhead shelves, I have a collection of gorillas, which stems from when I first started working at [my previous job]. Somebody was having a hard time pronouncing my [last] name, and I said, "Oh, it's easy . . . it rhymes with gorilla." And the minute I said that, I thought, "Oh, I should not have said this." And for the next few years, I was known as Mrs. Gorilla. So, I started collecting gorillas because of Mrs. Gorilla. . . . And I have a bunch of Cubs stuff because I'm a big Chicago Cubs fan. And then in the middle of it all hangs my graduation cap. I don't have a wall because I have a cubicle. I don't have a wall where I can hang my diploma. Like, a lot of supervisors have offices where their diplomas hang. Well, I don't have that. So, I hang my cap to remind me that I graduated, that I achieved an important dream.

PERFORMING THE DIALOGIC SELF

One of the primary goals of decorating one's cap is to be able to share something about oneself in the ritual space of the commencement ceremony. One graduate, Alena, offered this explanation of why she thought the practice of decorating mortarboards was so popular, echoing sentiments I encountered in many of the conversations I had with graduates:

> I think at the end of—like, once you've finished, you've been through college and it's just, it's definitely a journey. And once you've hit that finish line, I don't know, you kind of sit there and you realize, oh, okay, I've worked so hard for this and now I'm here. And I think at that moment, I don't know, I think it's just a really unique way of being able to express yourself. There's a lot of people there at graduation who are graduating either with different degrees or with the same degree that you are too, but you want to stand out. And I think personally, being able to decorate your own cap, just kind of gives you your own voice in the midst of that huge crowd.

The examples presented in the introduction focused primarily on graduates using their caps to perform social—or relational—selves, where the processes of decoration or display marked group affiliations or important relationships. These, however, are not the only facets of self that graduates put on display. Graduates also use their mortarboard displays to highlight key characteristics of themselves, including formative experiences, values, and ways of being in the world (e.g., persistent, resilient, positive, not taking oneself too seriously).

What constitutes the self, of course, is not static; it is multifaceted and ever-evolving.[2] This makes it difficult for some people to decide what aspect of themselves they want to foreground, which is evident in one graduate's explanation of why she decided *not* to decorate her cap. In addition to expressing a desire for her appearance to be traditional, citing the historical roots of the graduation ceremony, she explained:

> If I were to decorate my cap, I would decorate it with something that is important to me. There are numerous aspects of my life that hold significant importance; therefore, I didn't decorate because I didn't want to exclude certain parts of my life (for example, I have two kids, a husband, I love to run marathons, I love biology and sociology, etc. . . . how do I fit all of these "things" on a small graduation cap?). Third, I don't ever want to look back at my graduation pictures and think, "What was I thinking putting THAT on my cap!" (Think of a bad tattoo that some get when they are 18 that they end up regretting later in life).

For those who do decide to decorate their caps, the aspects of self that *are* presented in mortarboard displays are the results of choices made by individuals, choices that are shaped not only by the intentions of the graduate, but also by practical constraints (e.g., what will or will not fit on the cap, availability or cost of materials) as well as audience expectations. My interviews with graduates indicate that there are different audiences envisioned in the process of decorating one's cap, including their families, their friends, their fellow graduates, strangers who might benefit from their message, an amorphous anonymous public, and the individuals themselves—both in the present and in the future.

Similar to other genres of material culture like scrapbooks, quilts, yard art, and home altars, the decorated mortarboard is a complex genre that "corrals and contextualizes other discrete forms" (Christensen 2016, 46; Bakhtin et al. 1986). Meanings of these discrete forms are not inherent or self-evident; they are constructed in dialogue with others. In other words, these acts of individual expression are inherently relational, exemplifying Bakhtin's notion of the dialogic nature of discourse (Bakhtin and Holquist 1981). While Bakhtin wrote primarily about language and literature, his ideas are applicable to other domains of creative expression. As Deborah

Figure 2.1. Like scrapbooks, another material genre of personal expression, mortarboard displays curate an assemblage of discrete textual, visual, and material forms that carry significant meanings for the graduate. Photo credit: Sheila Bock.

J. Haynes asserts, "nearly all art is answerable in the sense that it evolves in relation to history and historical artifacts, to personal experience and reflection, and to identifiable formal issues" (Haynes 2008, 296).

Consider the cap of one graduate, a daughter of immigrants, that proclaimed, "This Xicana from El Chuco. ¡Si pudo!" (see figure 2.1). She explained, "It's bilingual, first of all. I speak both Spanish and English. And El Chuco is El Paso. It's like slang, what they call El Paso. And Xicana, well, you know, I'm Mexican and Panamanian, but I was born here, so that's what it represents to me." In describing her process of putting her cap together, she told me:

> I decorated it myself. I got the stickers from a Latino shop that sells Latino stickers, so I have little representations—the coffee, the Mexican bread, and the flowers. The white flowers actually represent Selena Quintanilla. . . . I love Selena, and white roses are her favorite, so that's why I chose the white roses as well. Because I'm from Texas. I grew up in Texas, in El Paso, a border city, and there's a really large influence of Selena there, so I kind of just mixed all that up together.

Acts of individual expression, be they textual, visual, material, or some other form in the folk assemblage (Santino 1986) of the decorated graduation cap, are both unique (in that they emerge within specific places and times that are not repeatable) and dialogic, always responsive to other acts of expression and their social, historical, and ideological contexts.

VIGNETTE #3

As graduation drew near in the spring of 2017, Abigail knew she wanted to decorate her cap, but she couldn't decide whether to display a message that was funny or a message that was meaningful. Ultimately, she decided to have two different decorated mortarboards:

> I would have the funny one for the pictures that I wanted, but then I would have something a little more serious and nicer to actually wear to my graduation ceremony. . . . So, for the funny one, my favorite meme that was really relevant at that time was the "Ted Cruz is the Zodiac Killer" joke that was floating around the Internet. . . . There was a period of, like, four months where probably every other thing I posted on Twitter was the "Ted Cruz is the Zodiac Killer" joke or reposting pictures, and I was probably way too into it. . . . And I thought it would be hilarious to do that, like really classy with black sparkly construction paper and nice cursive stickers, and have it look really nice and like something that would be serious, but then have it say, "Ted Cruz is the Zodiac Killer." . . . And then for the more serious meaningful one, I was actually really proud of the fact that I had gotten a math degree, because in high school, I was really bad at math, so I wanted it to reflect that. And then I also wanted it to be—I was in a fraternal organization through band that was really important to me so I did another one with black sparkly construction paper with fancy stickers that said, "Math is nice, but music charms the soul," which is a phrase that was associated with that band organization that I was in. . . . I had come into college as a music major, so I wanted to pay homage to that, that even though I hadn't finished that degree, I was in band for all four years, and that's something I continued to do. So, it was really an important part of my life that wasn't just what my degree was in.

For Abigail, decorating her caps served first and foremost as a form of self-expression: "This is a chance for me to show my college experience and what matters to me right now, and have a way to have some individuality in my graduation ceremony where we all look the same . . . so, it was, like, my friends and family are here. I've worked really hard for this, so I want to stand out a little bit and have it be, like, 'Yes, there are thousands of us here, but this is mine.'"

VIGNETTE #4

On the flat surface of the top of their mortarboard, Desiré affixed a square piece of white poster board that featured different words in different colors, presented in the style of a word cloud, including "feminist," "queer," "transformational," "muxerista," "resilience," "libre," "radical love," "nepantla," "decolonize," and "healing" (see figure 2.2).

"I had an assignment when I first started out in my [gender and sexuality studies] degree," they explained to me in 2018, "about wrapping up what I learned about social justice and feminism . . . and I actually went to that assignment and gathered some of the words that were written on there. And so I just wrote down the ones that just kept coming up throughout that degree."

The significance of their degree extended beyond what they learned academically:

> For a long time, I didn't really have any guidance or mentorship. I'm first generation, so it was kind of me trying to figure out a lot on my own. . . . It wasn't until I really got into my degree that I finally found community [in college]. And that's why it was really important for me to write [those words] on top, [to show how the gender and sexuality studies major] provided me with opportunities and community. . . . I'm so grateful for having been able to grow as a person and to name my lived experiences, and to put words and meanings to what I had experienced as a person of color in the US. . . . This degree means much more than just getting a college degree. It gave me an opportunity to understand myself, understand the communities I'm a part of, and understand what transformative change I want to see in the world, and how I can engage in that.[3]

The top of their cap also included their name, Desiré:

> My name's included in there because I think my name has been really important, even just the pronunciation of this. I was being called, like, "Dez-uh-ray" for a really long time in my life [instead of "De-see-rréh"]. And that was because—so, English is not my first language, and that's how they [English speakers] said my name. And I was like, "Okay, that's my name, I guess." But that's never how my parents have said my name. And so when I was in college and took a Spanish course, the professor said it the way my name has always been said. And it was just such a moment to me . . . I was like, "Oh my God, that's my name" . . . and so that's one thing that happened in college that gave me agency to say, "This is my name, and I'm going to ask you to say my name in the way that it's supposed to be pronounced." The way that those who named me meant for it to be pronounced.[4]

Desiré chose the materials they used very intentionally: "I had [reflective paper] that I got from a package that came with some healing material—some sage [and crystals] and stuff like that. So I thought it would be nice to put it on top and have that, the essence of cleaning out what has been and starting something new. . . . I thought maybe it would bring the same energy with the words, manifesting the words and manifesting this really important moment."

Hanging off the sides of the cap were several smaller pieces of paper, each of which included an image and text from a popular Internet meme.

> A lot of the memes [hanging down on the side] are just kind of describing my hesitation about being in academia and just, like what does it mean to graduate? And using humor to get through the anxieties and the fear that I felt. . . . [Looking back on my experiences in academia], it was really hard at some points . . . I didn't even want to walk [at commencement]. I did it for other people who wanted me to do it. And so, that was my way of also just helping me get through it. . . . Which is not to say that I didn't appreciate my degree. And that's kind of what I wanted to reflect at the top—that I learned so much and it gave me so many opportunities. But like I said, I'm still kind of recovering from what it's meant to be in college.

When I asked them to elaborate, they told me: "There's a lot of stigma and shame that comes with mental health. And I think also physical disabilities, and especially if they're invisible and you're not able to really address them up front with people, disclosing that to people and to also then the institution, and not getting the support that you thought you were going to get. It was really hard to go through that."

They went on to explain why they decided to include humor in the design of their cap: "I think [incorporating humor into my cap] was important for me because that was the way that me and my friends were able to get through the hard times. We'd just kind of make jokes and laugh about it. And we would have, obviously, serious conversations, but in those moments where it just seems too hard to have those conversations because we're not necessarily in the mental space, it was a lot easier for us to engage online about how others were feeling the same way as us. I guess maybe it made us feel less alone in that process."

Their ambivalence about the process of getting to graduation informed how they selected and situated the memes they included: "On one side, I wanted to put the ones that spoke to how I was really struggling.[5] And on the other side, I wanted to put the memes that demonstrated that I was so excited and happy to be able to graduate and to move on to a different

Figure 2.2. Decorated mortarboards are complex, multimodal performances of self that can reference multiple personal experiences and perspectives at the same time. Photo credit: Desiré Galvez.

chapter in my life."[6] The placement of the memes carried an additional meaning as well: "The reason why they're dangling [is] because it reminded me of a sombrero where they have the little things hanging off the sides . . . I hung them that way to represent my Mexican lineage and identity."

MEDIA INTERTEXTUALITY IN MATERIAL PRESENTATIONS OF SELF

One recurring and consistently prevalent theme I have observed in my documentation of this mortarboard tradition is the integration of popular culture references (both textual and visual) into the material performances of self in the mortarboard displays. In other words, many of the caps illustrate what Mark Allen Peterson terms media intertextuality, defined as "the interweaving of bits and pieces of dialogue, actions, or other symbols from mass media texts into everyday speech and action" (2005, 130). Building on foundational work in sociolinguistics that approaches intertextuality as an active social process of decontextualization and recontextualization (Bauman and Briggs 1990; Briggs and Bauman 1992; Silverstein and Urban

1996), Peterson argues for media intertextuality to be understood not just as a characteristic of texts but as social action:

> People are never *only* audiences constructing readings of [media] texts, they also seize upon, remember, replicate, and transform elements from the media they consume. They quote dialogue, emulate styles, and whistle tunes they learned from television, radio, or the movies. . . . People become performers of text, and they also become producers of text, weaving elements from the media they have consumed into new narratives and artifacts that can be displayed to construct particular forms of sociality. (Peterson 2005, 130)

While the recontextualization of media texts is certainly not the only form of intertextual engagement in mortarboard displays, attending to how graduates use these discursive resources to craft presentations of self makes visible the inherently dialogic nature of this process.

Many people who choose to decorate their caps seek to make selected life experiences visible to their audiences. On a practical level, media discourse provides opportunities to do this in the limited space that the mortarboard provides, for as Peterson explains, "people who dwell in media-saturated societies are expected to know about an extensive series of media genres, storyworlds, and mediated figures beyond their face-to-face social experiences" (Peterson 2005, 133). Given this expectation, many graduates use media discourse to signify key elements of their personal story, personal philosophy, or personality and make them legible to public audiences that do not necessarily know them. In other words, the integration of media discourse creates opportunities to align oneself (and one's story) with characters and narrative plot lines from popular culture.

One 2018 graduate included the words "what like it's hard?" in pink letters on her cap, adding in white lettering on the bottom edges: "Harvard Law 2021." With this textual reference to the 2001 film *Legally Blonde*, this honors student—who was blonde—explained that she wanted to communicate something about both her personality and where she was going: Harvard Law School in the fall, just like the film's bubbly, smart, and underestimated main character, Elle Woods.

We see similar alignments with the incorporation of song lyrics, as many graduates use these texts to index life experiences and/or views on life. In one example, a graduate decorated her cap with a large image of the musical artist Nicki Minaj, along with a line from the 2017 song "MotorSport": "You see the stats you know what I am about!" (see figure 2.3). "A lot of people doubted me that I was even going to be able to get out of high

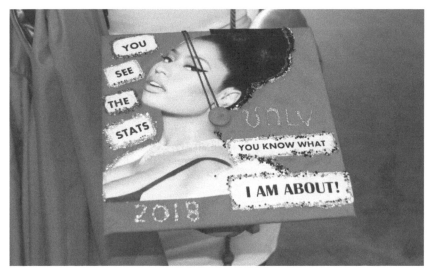

Figure 2.3. Graduates often use media texts as discursive resources in their crafted presentations of self. Photo credit: Sheila Bock.

school," the graduate explained, "so graduating college is a big accomplishment for me . . . [my mortarboard is] showing people that my track record can prove it for you. I don't have to say anything."

Another graduate adorned her cap with lyrics from Simple Plan's 2007 song "When I'm Gone": "Leave the past in the past, gonna find the future." "The song lyrics mean the world to me," she wrote in her survey response. "After high school, my mom and I found ourselves homeless and living on the street. Those lyrics inspired me to take initiative to leave my past behind me and pursue higher education. . . . I wouldn't have been a student in a university without that song inspiring me to push through my homelessness and apply."

In his discussion of media intertextuality, Peterson further explains how "knowledge of particular kinds of media texts and an ability to display this knowledge competently is a form of cultural capital valued in many social fields" (Peterson 2005, 130). Strategic uses of this media knowledge can work to make the public audiences "smaller" or more intimate through inside jokes—references not everybody would get—as in the case of one graduate I talked to whose cap featured the text: "May your caps fly as high as your dreams!" Referencing the words of the fictional character Michael Scott from the television show *The Office*, she told me that she likes the idea that the quote looks really sweet if you don't know where it is coming from, but it's actually a really funny joke. When I asked her if many people she talked to recognized the reference, she answered that about 50 percent did.

Figure 2.4. The image macro is a digital folklore genre that is commonly integrated into the mortarboard designs. Photo credit: Sheila Bock.

Another graduate included a reference to a Bible verse alongside the words "B.A. chemistry." Her cap also included visual representations of chemistry lab equipment to highlight her degree, along with multiple blue jewels. As she explained during an interview, people who watched the television show *Breaking Bad* would understand the reference—specifically, the visual reference to "blue sky," the blue-colored pure crystal meth manufactured by the chemistry teacher Walter White and his partner in crime Jesse Pinkman in the fictional world of the show.

Peterson's explanation of media intertextuality focuses on mass media texts, but we also see examples of new media texts being recontextualized into mortarboard displays, particularly popular Internet memes. By far the most prevalent Internet meme genre I encountered on decorated graduation caps was the image macro, a genre characterized by an image with a witty caption (see figure 2.4). The four-sided shape of the mortarboard lends itself extremely well to the materialization of this digital folklore genre, a genre that is meant to be re-presented and adapted to different situations and shared with public audiences (Grundlingh 2018).

The primary goal of many of the graduates who integrate popular memes into their designs is to be funny. This juxtaposition works to stand in contrast to, and therefore push back against, the formality and reverence typically characterizing the commencement event, as in the case of Abigail (introduced in Vignette #3), who sought to emphasize this contrast by presenting the "goofy" phrase "Ted Cruz is the Zodiac Killer" in a "really classy" way. The intent of humor, to be clear, is not always understood by graduates as being at odds with the overall goals of graduation, which include celebrating a major accomplishment. Graduate Ryan's cap featured a large image of actor Shia LaBeouf with a thought bubble coming out of his head that read, "I did it!," referencing LaBeouf's popular fake TED Talk that became the source of many parodies circulating online. In explaining why he decorated his cap the way he did, Ryan explained: "The video itself was a joke but as you watch it and finish it, it is kind of motivational in a weird way. He only says like 7 different words throughout the entire video but it means a lot and I guess it kind of resonated with me. He tells you in the video, 'Just keep doing it, do it do it do it.' And we did it, we graduated, so that's why I picked it."

In thinking about media intertextuality as social action, it is important to think beyond the *content* of the specific media texts being referenced to the *generic* meanings being indexed through the acts of performance. Peterson reminds us, for example, how "children quickly learn that teachers reward literary forms of intertextuality but frown on intertextual play that embeds television and film texts into schoolwork" (Peterson 2005, 136). It is notable, then, that so many decorated caps integrate text and imagery from these and other "low brow" genres of popular culture, especially during a ritual ceremony marked by formality, reverence, and the celebration of academic values. In other words, it is not just the content of the popular culture references but the indexing of these genres in this space that works to push back against the formality of the occasion. And as Desiré's words in Vignette #4 make clear, in addition to communicating something about oneself (one's humor, one's knowledge of new media, one's perspectives on the process of attaining higher education), the inclusion of Internet memes into the design of one's graduation cap can also work to draw connections to other contexts where these memes are shared (online with friends) and to the sociability these contexts engender (seeking out community to help cope with the stress and feelings of alienation that the pursuit of higher education can bring).

VIGNETTE #5

Amara,[7] with the help of a good friend, adorned the top of her cap with a glittery piece of scrapbook paper and pearls around the edges. Against this background, she used glittery golden letters to write, "to God be the glory."

"I'm very involved in my church, and I got involved four years ago . . . right after high school graduation. So I've grown a lot spiritually since then and it's really been a big part of who I am in my life . . . and I thought the cap was a really good way of showing that." When I asked her to explain how she has seen herself grow over the last four years, she responded:

> When I say growth over the years, it really is a lot of different areas in my life. To begin with, growth in terms of spirituality, because four years ago, meaning when I was in high school, I was involved in my church. I would go to church on Sundays and stuff, but never really understood that having—when they say that spark in your heart, or having that fire for something, I never felt that or had that before. I think I just didn't invest that much time into reading the Bible and getting really in touch with other believers as well, like in my church. And so after high school happened and I graduated, and I remember that during that summer, I ended up going to church more often and, so, I grew spiritually from that. And the experiences that I've had being in college over the four years. I'm definitely not the same person that I was before spiritually, so I really wanted to show that. And second, I grew in terms of professionalism and in my field [public health], because I did a lot of different internships, got involved. Really tried to find out, like, why am I in this field and why do I care about it so much? And in that sense I've grown, but also personally, I think. I know my values and I wanted to show what I hold true to myself, bringing positivity and just having, like, good vibes I think overall. I've grown in those ways, and just figuring out what my values are [and] standing firm in my faith.

When Amara first decided to decorate her cap, she knew she wanted to do something that related to her faith, though it took her a while to figure out exactly what she wanted to do:

> It was so hard, actually . . . I have a few different favorite quotes, biblical verses that I like. And most of them just were too long to put on my cap. And so, I'm like, okay, I need to find something that represents what I'm—you know, that I want to give glory but I also want to put, you know . . . something that means something to me, and they were just all too long to actually put a verse on there from the Bible. And so, I just ended up, you know, after I looked at a couple of different verses, I just sat there thinking like, honestly, the only thing that I can put on there—I love all these verses and they mean something to me because of, you know, what had happened for whatever that verse holds in my life—I just felt like all I could do was thank God. And I played around with the wording a little bit. Like, you know, I remember putting, "Thank you, Lord," or just "Glory to You." But I just, at the end of the day, I started looking up, I was on Pinterest and I started looking at, "Praise God" or "Glory to God" for graduation caps, like getting ideas. And I saw one that had, "To God Be the Glory." That is perfect.

At the ceremony itself, she had friends who asked her why she put that message on her cap. In recounting this, she explained:

> It gives me so much joy when someone even asks me that because it allows me to reflect back on these four years. And I kind of try to refer back to the Bible, especially if they kind of are on the same path, too, and they get it. And so I'll tell them . . . I can tell this person this and that, and this is what that means, where for other people I just kind of talk about how grateful I've been and how I've had a great experience in my college years.

She continued:

> To be honest, I didn't want to take credit for just everything that has happened, because I think that's the easiest for us to do as human beings. I know when something good happens, or I make it somewhere, I'm always like, "Yes, I did it." But more than anything, I know I have to give glory to God, who I know is my Lord. And so in that sense, I wanted to show it on there because I don't want people to just be cheering for *me*. Like my family, my friends who were there to support me, saying like, "You did it." You know, "You're here, and you're onto the next step." That's great, and I love all of that support. But at the same time, it was a reminder for me, but also for everybody there that was there to support me, that it was not just *me* alone who did it to get there. It was, you know, it was God's glory and mercy in my life that got me here, and I wanted that to be the centerpiece and something that I would carry around with me during graduation and even at the after party we had. "What is this cap?" You know, and I kept explaining it to people, like, "Glory to God," "Glory to God," but I have this cap with me that I'm wearing and I'm holding. And so, I thought I wanted to make sure that that was a big part of what we were celebrating with my family.

When I asked about her decision to include the pearls, Amara likened her inclusion of the pearls to dressing up, giving respect to the written message featured on her cap: "With the Orthodox Christian church . . . every time we go to church on Sundays, it's always you wear the Ethiopian traditional clothing. So, it's very fancy, like a dress. . . . So, I'm used to that. You know, when you think about going to church it's supposed to be, you know, a very sacred and honored place." She explained that the incorporation of pearls into her design was meant to show that she valued the mortarboard and the accomplishment it represented: "I really wanted to make it elegant, and I think to me, pearls have always represented something elegant. . . . And so, I wanted to make sure the pearls were something that I have all around the border, just to show this is something elegant or something that you value."

VIGNETTE #6

When Christa walked at her commencement, the top of her graduation cap was adorned with spikes—"big silver spikes that you would see on someone's motorcycle jacket" (see figure 2.5). "I'm very interested in the punk subculture," she explained, "and I have kind of been active within that community for, oh man, I don't know, probably since I was 14 or 15. And the music and the political activism stance and the do-it-yourself mentality have all been things that have resonated with me since I was a teenager." Describing how her appreciation of the punk culture developed as she got older, she said:

> At first, you're a teenager and you think it's cool to say, "Eff you" to everybody and, you know, act kind of like an ass, but it becomes more meaningful and you understand the purpose as you get older. So, for me, a lot of times with the punk subculture, you'll find that people put studs and spikes on their leather jackets or their denim jackets that they kind of customize. . . . It's just something you really see a lot of . . . where it started in the '70s and '80s, there was just a lot of political and social turmoil, and a lot of just unrest within people. And a lot of anger and a lot of, you know, willingness to do better. And wanting to do better for yourself and for society and kind of rejecting all these things that we thought were the norm, and rejecting all of the -isms . . . and of course, that's always been something that was important to me. But I also really, when I was a lot younger, I also just liked the fact of being able to make people angry or, you know, seeing that I *do* have a voice and I *can* get a reaction out of people. But as I grew older, I realized that, you know, you can use that voice to be obnoxious and to stand out, but you can also use that voice to do a lot of good. And I think that's kind of at the crux of what it meant to be a punk, for real, and not just wanting to be a punk to look cool and scare your neighbors.[8]

When I asked her why it made sense for her to reference that punk subculture on her mortarboard when she walked for graduation, she responded:

> That's a big part of my personal identity and a big part of, honestly, what even got me through college. I really feel like I'm a workaholic and, you know, being part of that subculture was something that allowed me to have time to relax or to kind of let loose. Or you know, really be myself and not like my "academic" self all of the time, or not stressing about school. Like, I would go to shows and I wouldn't think about school at all, which is completely rare for me because I'm always up in my head. But that's kind of the one place where I really felt like I could be myself and not worry about being perfect. And so, having that reprieve was really, really

Figure 2.5. Some graduates use the space of the mortarboard to highlight, and thus "remain true" to, aspects of the self that may at first glance seem at odds with the persona of the successful student. Photo credit: Sheila Bock.

valuable and got me through school. But I feel like you also get lost in the sea of people at graduation. Because everyone looks the same and we're all wearing the same ugly red stuff. And so—actually, my friends were joking that that's the most color they've ever seen me wear. Which is probably true, but—but you do kind of lose yourself there. . . . I don't want to lose myself, you know, to school or to a profession, or to a larger society that tells me that I have to follow X, Y, Z patterns, and this is the way it's supposed to be. So, this is kind of my way of saying like, yes, I did do, quote/unquote, the "right thing" by going to college, but I did it for me, and I did it with my future in mind, and I'm still going to remain true to that image of myself.

"I think for me," she reflected, "it symbolized that I didn't really have to give myself up in the process of going to college."

PERFORMING THE SELF THROUGH DRESS

Dress, in the words of folklorist Carrie Hertz, is an "integrated part of lived experience, something that serves multiple needs for personal agency and creativity" (Hertz 2013, 4). While everyday dress certainly fulfills these functions, special occasion dress, particularly bodily adornment associated with ritual events such as weddings, quinceañeras, or commencement ceremonies, provides opportunities for heightened displays of self. As noted in the introduction, the whole assemblage of graduation dress (e.g., what is worn under the uniform gown and hidden from view; what shoes, jewelry, and other visible accessories are worn; the styling of hair and makeup) functions communicatively within the ritual space of commencement. Even the choice *not* to decorate one's cap functions in this way, for as Pravina Shukla reminds us, "to choose to look like everybody else—to remain as inconspicuous, as conventional as possible—is a decision no less willed than the decision to be a star of the fashion avant-garde" (Shukla 2008, 384).

As a highly visible form of bodily adornment within the space of the ceremony, the embellishment of the mortarboard is shaped by the stylistic and aesthetic preferences of the individual wearing it. This preference might be to avoid "being plain," as one graduate told me, or "to stand out but not be over the top," in the words of another, or to show a coordinated attention to detail, as in the case of one graduate who spent several days bedazzling her cap to match her sparkly shoes.

Several graduates interviewed for this project integrated references to different forms of dress into the design of their caps, drawing on the meanings these material forms carried, as well as the different social and historical contexts they indexed, in their efforts to transform the mortarboard into a site of personal expression. Amara, introduced in Vignette #5, used pearls to index other contexts of dressing up and to affirm and visually cue her respect for the formality of the occasion. References to other contexts of dress were also used to highlight aspects of identity that graduates wanted represented on their caps. At times, these references were subtle, as in the case of Desiré, introduced in Vignette #4, whose placement of multiple memes hanging off the sides of their mortarboard was intended to reference a sombrero, a marker of their Mexican identity. Other times, the indexical references were more overt. One graduate, a veteran, integrated her dog tag and fabric from the last uniform she wore before she retired from the military (as part of an assemblage that also included the United States flag and a three-dimensional cupcake representing her work as a pastry chef; see figure 2.6).

Another graduate, Cassidy, who was born in Hawaii and graduating from UNLV, integrated flowers into the design of her cap to reference a haku lei. As she explained to me in 2018:

> I'm mostly Filipino but I grew up in Hawaii. And you know, it's a tradition for your family to give you leis and all that kind of stuff on your graduation. And they also have a haku lei, which goes around your head. It's sort of like a crown of flowers that they used to wear in traditional Hawaii. And so, I was kind of inspired by that idea . . . I thought it would

Figure 2.6. Dress is a powerful form of communication, and the meanings carried by different forms of dress and bodily adornment (in this case, a military dog tag and fatigues) are often integrated into the designs of decorated mortarboards. Photo credit: Sheila Bock.

be awesome to respect where I came from on this momentous day. And a lot of my family flew out from Hawaii, and I knew it was something that was really important for them to see me graduate, and it was important to me as well. And I guess it also was just kind of, I just wanted to remember always where I came from, you know?

Another graduate, a history major, modeled the design of his cap after a Victorian era military uniform as a way to pay tribute to what he enjoyed learning about as he earned his degree:

My main focus of study is British history and the British Empire in the 19th and 20th centuries, so I really wanted to do something kind of Victorian-ish. So I looked up a picture of old Victorian military uniforms, and I modeled it after one of Prince Albert's uniforms from the TV show *Victoria*. And I basically used some gold tape, some construction paper, some steam punk wall prints and some gears to give it a little bit of an edge, and of course glitter, 'cause you gotta have glitter, right? . . . I mainly wanted it to be symbolic of what I did here [at the university] and the things I loved devoting my time to.

The caps of other graduates illustrate "an overarching personal style that prevails despite shifts of scene," or what Pravina Shukla terms "traditions of the self" (Shukla 2008, 262), as in the case of Christa, introduced in Vignette #6, who decorated her cap to align with the punk aesthetic exhibited in her everyday dress. For Christa, bringing the punk aesthetic into the ritual space of commencement became a way of communicating that, while at first glance they might appear at odds with one another, the version of herself indexed by the black background and silver spikes was not incompatible with the version of herself indexed by the mortarboard (or the ribbon adorned with the words "M.S. coming in 2019"). One did not diminish the significance of the other.

VIGNETTE #7

Mariana did not decorate her cap until the night before her graduation ceremony, in part because she was not sure exactly what she wanted to do:

> I actually went to Michael's and I bought like $40 worth of things because I didn't know what I wanted to put on it. So, I was like, I made sure that I had all the letters in case I wanted to do all these different things . . . I'd always joked about putting "#FUCKICE" on it because I'd always wanted to do that. And it was just kind of my way of really, like, you know, I hate everything that's happening, all the things I'm fighting for. And that's a hashtag that I very much believe in because there's been so much damage done to undocumented people through ICE [Immigration and Customs Enforcement] . . . I joked even with my little sister last year. I was like, "I'm gonna do it. I'm gonna put lights on the words so everyone can see it, even when they turn the lights off." I was so, I was so there for that but I don't know . . . eventually I kind of felt like, oh, I'll put a Hamilton quote like Sara [introduced in Vignette #8] did . . . and then, even up until the very last day, I had thought I was going to put "Immigrants, We Get the Job Done." It was something that I had all the letters for. Like, I bought all the letters just to do that, but then I got to actually putting them on the page and I realized that I wanted to put something more personal, something more related to being undocumented because it's such a salient, I guess, identity for me . . . so I ended up putting, "Love Has No Borders," which is something I also saw a lot of on the inspiration blogs that I follow for grad caps, like on Instagram. And for a long time I was looking at what I wanted to do, and I sat down with friends and we went through tags, and took pictures of everything. I made quotes from books that I really like. Honestly, I put so much thought into it, but at the end of the day, I think "Love Has No Borders" was something that I could see my mom really liking. I feel like she would be really mad at me if I did put "#FUCKICE," which is eventually why I didn't do it.

In addition to considering how her mom would respond, Mariana considered what kind of message *she* wanted to display: "And I think in myself, too, I felt like I guess I could [put #FUCKICE], but I feel that would be like giving too much attention to ICE. I don't know. Like, in a way, it is defiance but at the same time, this is *my* accomplishment, right? This is me. This is what *I* did. I'm going to put something that's positive, something that's about me, right? 'Love Has No Borders,' eventually that's what I ended up with. And my mom was happy about that because, you know, it's beautiful."

Describing what she liked about the phrase "love has no borders" for her cap, she said, "I think it's really paying tribute to everything that my parents did for me in this journey, because ultimately, 'Love Has No Borders,' it really is a relationship between them and I, right? Like love had no borders when they decided to love me enough to give me a better life."

She had an often-contentious relationship with members of her family, causing her to move out while she was a student, though as graduation neared, their relationship began to improve:

> I think I became very soft towards the end, which is something that I haven't been able to do for a long time, and being vulnerable with those feelings and being open to my family about how I felt and how sad I felt about everything. So, I think at the end of the day, me choosing "Love Has No Borders" over "#FUCKICE" meant that vulnerability, right? Like I could say "#FUCKICE" but then I'd be the way that I've always been this entire time, just that anger pushing me forward. And that's okay, right? Sometimes that's okay. But I think especially for this, taking into account my entire trajectory . . . not just college but everything before that—high school, and middle school, and elementary school, my parents getting me through all that, really it comes down to love has no borders. Before I even knew what ICE was, I knew that love had no borders, right? So, that's kind of what it comes down to.

She further reflected on the options she was choosing between:

> There's strength in that "#FUCKICE" . . . but I think at the end of that day, I need to be genuine with myself and in everything that I do. In some way it *had* to be about immigration. That was just true to me. And so, in that way, I didn't feel like I was doing it for anybody other than myself. And I think when it came down to "#FUCKICE" versus "Love Has No Borders," that was really a very personal decision, because I know I could have dealt with "#FUCKICE" with my family. They would have gotten over it eventually, right? But it was also a little bit more personal in that

sense. And so, honestly, whatever I would have put on my grad cap, I think it would have still been true to who I am. . . . I think I shared [the message that I did] eventually because it gave me strength, so I thought maybe it will give other people strength, you know, to know that you can be open about your status, and you can be open about the fact that you want a positive outcome for our immigrant community.

VIGNETTE #8

Sara played around with different ideas for decorating her mortarboard. She seriously considered featuring a quote from the coming-of-age novel *Aristotle and Dante Discover the Secrets of the Universe* by Benjamin Saenz, a book she first read during her second year in college in a class on young adult literature. "It's about two queer Mexican boys coming of age and figuring out their identities in El Paso in the '60s," she explained. "It changed my perspective on so many things. I recently reread it at the beginning of this semester as well, and I went through and highlighted the book with my favorite quotes."

She also considered different quotes from the musical *Hamilton*, including "history has its eyes on you," "immigrants, we get the job done," and "rise up." Ultimately, she decided on the quote "rise up." "I have this long history with *Hamilton*," she told me. "Since high school, I've been kind of following it. I remember when Lin-Manuel Miranda first performed his demo tape for the intro of *Hamilton* at the slam poetry event that [President Barack] Obama hosted. And I was like, 'Oh, that's so cool,' because at that time, I was in American history and [Alexander] Hamilton was actually one of my favorite political history characters. So I was like, 'Oh, that's so cool.' Like, someone else figured out that Hamilton's kind of an interesting historical figure because he very much was."

After the hit musical debuted on Broadway and became a cultural phenomenon, her friend introduced her to the soundtrack while they were on a road trip together, and she described listening to it for the first time as "an experience." She also recalled listening to the soundtrack "non-stop" as she wrote papers for her college classes. While each of the quotes she considered had some kind of special meaning for her, her final choice of "rise up" was heavily informed by practical and aesthetic considerations—specifically, what would fit in the small space of the cap and what would look the best.

During her brainstorming process, she talked to her mom about the different quotes she was considering, because her mom's opinion mattered a lot to her:

So, I was running some quotes by her, and I think the full quote I was considering putting on there was, "When You're Down on Your Knees, Rise Up" . . . and it ended up getting condensed to just "Rise Up," because it looked the best. And I didn't have that many letters. But [my mom] was like, "Oh, I really like that. I really like that. Where's that from? Is it from the Bible?" . . . We are a Christian family, she raised me very much like that, and I am—I don't say religious, I say spiritual, right? So, I'm like, "Oh no, it's not. It's from the *Hamilton* musical I've been telling you about." She's like, "Oh, well, did they get that from the Bible?" I'm like, "No, I think it just means—I mean—I mean, you can see it that way, Mama. There's no reason you cannot interpret it that way." Because that's true. You know, when you're down on your knees, you rise up. That's like just a general proverb that a lot of people can understand, whether you're religious or not. So, she ended up really liking that one, and I think that's why I stuck with that, because it resonates on various fronts. I read it, and I automatically know it's from *Hamilton* because I'm so into [the musical]. But other people, they would be like, "Oh, is that from a proverb?" or "Is that from the Bible?" or "Is that from, like, an inspirational quote?" . . . So that worked very nicely with the cap. I didn't want something so specific that people don't understand the reference, so that one worked out very well.

Sara decorated her cap with her friend, Mariana (introduced in Vignette #7), who purchased the supplies they used. Some of these supplies included monarch butterflies, which they both incorporated into the design of their caps: "[Mariana] wanted the monarch butterflies on hers," Sara told me, "which are a symbol of immigration, and positivity, and reform . . . so I shared the butterflies with her." Sara was also pleased with how, because she and Mariana designed their caps using the same materials and letters of the same font, their two caps looked good together as they stood side by side. While they did not coordinate their individual designs explicitly, there was some visual consistency between them that she appreciated.

MEDIATING THE RECEPTION OF SELVES ON DISPLAY

Approaching these mortarboard displays as performances—classically defined in folklore studies as an "assumption of responsibility to an audience for a display of communicative competence" (Bauman 1977, 293)—opens up the question of what makes for a "successful" performance. Graduates I have talked to have identified several markers of evaluation from others that they used to assess the "success" of their performances, such as chuckles and nods of appreciation from strangers to indicate competent performances of humor; tears from family members to indicate competent

Figure 2.7. Facing the challenge of deciding what elements of the self to put on display, some graduates opt to decorate two mortarboards: one to wear for the commencement ceremony and one to wear for pictures to post on social media. Photo credit: Sheila Bock.

performances of sincere appreciation; and exclamations of "That's so you!" from close friends to indicate competent performances of self.

My interviews also reveal a clear awareness on the part of graduates of the "mixed audiences" (Buccitelli 2012, 77) for their mortarboard displays, where people representing different social spheres are participants in the same communicative event. Graduates in this setting, then, must also consider what makes for a successful performance when different audiences, each bringing different modes of evaluation, are envisioned.

Sara, introduced in Vignette #8, relied on the interpretive ambiguity of the phrase "Rise up!" to create a design that was both true to herself and accessible to her family. In cases where different goals and expectations don't align so easily in a single design, graduates must either choose to prioritize one mode of self-presentation over another (as we see with Mariana in Vignette #7) or create and execute two different designs (as we see with Abigail in Vignette #3; see also figure 2.7). One graduate I talked to even outsourced that decision-making process, posting different options on social media (one of which referenced her student debt) and asking for feedback. A self-described "Harry Potter nerd," she ultimately opted for what she termed "a more positive option"—a design featuring the phrase "accio diploma," a textual reference to the fictional world created by author J. K. Rowling.

Amid these different considerations and strategies of negotiation, though, the successful performance of self is paramount. For some, the

originality of the design is important, though for most of the graduates
I talked to, originality was not necessary for the decorated mortarboard
to be an accurate representation of oneself. Like other genres of material expression, decorated graduation cap designs are "freely available for
adaptation" (Christensen 2011, 198), and graduates often look online to get
ideas for how to decorate their caps. The process of adaptation, though,
always involves some form of personalization.

Often, this personalization is integrated into the design itself, in the
form of favorite colors, inside jokes, and alignments with the graduate's
sense of style in more everyday modes of dress. One graduate who adorned
her cap with gold, one of her favorite colors, and words that were important to her, including "love" and "family," proudly told me: "If you know
me, you'll be able to recognize that this is my cap. . . . It's me." Another
graduate utilized his skills as a graphic design major to put the cover of
Kanye West's *Graduation* album on his cap, with a portrait of his own head
photoshopped over it. Using this album cover "is a common way to do a
grad cap," he said, "but nobody else has done it like I did. It is me."

As with other material genres of personal display (Christensen 2016,
42–44), precisely *what* is being communicated (and to whom) is often mediated by the modes of display. Some graduates invite audience engagement
by embedding their designs with words or images whose meanings are not
quite apparent, recognizing (and often hoping) that this will initiate conversations. As one graduate explained in her survey response, "It added an
extra layer of fun, because I knew I would get questions about it."

The intersubjective nature of mortarboard displays also creates opportunities for graduates to manage the visibility of the experiences and perspectives they index in these public displays of the personal.[9] One graduate,
for example, adorned her cap with an image of the Beatles' *Abbey Road*
album cover she purchased from Amazon. When I asked her about her
design, she told me: "I love the Beatles. I grew up listening to the Beatles,
and my dad actually passed last year, so this is a nod to him. Dad was a
big Beatles fan, and he was a drummer all his life." Her decorative choices
carried layers of meaning (e.g., showing her appreciation for the Beatles,
indexing childhood experiences listening to the music of the Beatles,
memorializing her father), though not all of the meanings were meant to be
apparent to others. Indeed, unless people viewing her cap knew her father
well, the cap's connection to him could only be known through conversation with the graduate. The apparent legibility of the widely recognizable
Abbey Road album made it a kind of undercoded signifier, "dividing insiders
and outsiders in a way that avoids proclamations of secrecy in favor of an

Figure 2.8. Utilized as sites of strategic visibility, graduation caps create opportunities to engage in destigmatization and to be a source of affirmation and solidarity for those who have had similar experiences. Photo credit: Sheila Bock.

easy readability that deflects further scrutiny" (Christensen 2016, 82; see also Kirshenblatt-Gimblett 1998, 255). The same dynamics of managing visibility were at play with the inclusion of the *cempasúchil on* Brenda's cap (introduced in Vignette #1). In this way, it was at the graduate's discretion whether that dimension of meaning would be made public through individual conversations or hidden from view.

VIGNETTE #9

Set against a sparkly silver background, Isabel adorned her cap with an image of the ribbon for suicide awareness: a teal and purple ribbon, with teal birds flying out of the ribbon. Along the edge, she wrote the word "survivor" (see figure 2.8). "I've struggled with mental illness for my entire life," she told me in our January 2020 interview, "and it's been part of my family's history and story, and so that kind of motivated what I've been researching [for my senior capstone project], which was on my mind when I was graduating. But I chose that design in particular for my graduation cap because I had actually attempted suicide over the summer [a few months before I graduated]. And I was about, it was midway through my summer semester, so I had a semester and a half left. And had I been successful with that attempt, I wouldn't have been able to graduate. So, it was very much on my mind that I had made it so close and almost wasn't able to complete that part of my journey."

The public nature of the commencement ceremony heavily informed her decision to decorate her cap the way she did. Connecting her decorative choices to her career goals of working in the field of counseling, she explained: "I cannot move forward in my life and career saying that I am an advocate of ending stigma surrounding these issues if I am not willing to open up the door to talking about my own experiences with them." She also thought about the other people attending the ceremony who have struggled with similar issues: "If I saw that on someone's graduation cap, it would be comforting and affirming, and feel like a place of solidarity."

As a mental health advocate, she saw the commencement ceremony to be a particularly strong opportunity for advocacy:

> I think one of the reasons that I thought it was a great platform was that school is really stressful [*laughing*]. College can be a very difficult experience for a lot of different reasons. You know, you have the academic pressure. A lot of people are leaving home for the first time. You have a whole new social setting, different ways to make friends and engage with people. Like, it's just kind of a hotbed of stress [*laughing*]. So, I wanted to I guess be able to remind people that, you know, yes, this is a wonderful celebration and not only have you gotten through the academic side of it, but, you know, there are people who haven't been able to get through it because of mental health reasons, and everybody who is there and who is going through that process was able to make it through. And I think that's something that's important. You know, not just to acknowledge the academic achievement, but the personal growth and the necessity of mental health and, you know, mental wellness, that students have to achieve to be able to get through or at least, you know, [*laughing*] try to.

Turning more focused attention to the university setting, she explained:

> I think [mental health] is something that really isn't talked about in the wider conversation about higher education as much as it should be . . . those are conversations that aren't really had as much with incoming students in the way that would promote them reaching out and finding support, and utilizing the resources of the university. So, I think in that way, it just, I wanted to kind of say "Oh, hey, this is something that we should be focusing on and talking about and acknowledging as part of the successes and challenges that students face."

Isabel saw her cap as sharing a positive message, serving as a celebration of having survived her suicide attempt, though she noticed that her cap seemed to cause some unspoken discomfort for some of her family members:

> Obviously it's not a positive thing, but having the support and ability to get through that, not everybody has that. And so, I saw it as a celebration, but I understand that a lot of people [*laughing*], you know, don't really. And they only see the, you know, tragic end of it. And so, you know, I can definitely see how for a lot of people it's like, why are you bringing up this tragedy when you're supposed to be celebrating? And you know, I don't know that they knew how to grapple with that, because I don't think it really was in line with their narrative for commencement and their narrative for mental health awareness.

VIGNETTE #10

Ray did not walk at his university commencement in 1999, since the graduating class was so big and there would be no moment of individual recognition. Instead, he walked with three hundred to four hundred others at UCLA's Raza graduation ceremony, with a rainbow flag, a rainbow tassel around his neck, and a mortarboard adorned with a bouquet of real chrysanthemums. "I'm a gay Chicano man," he told me in 2018. In college, he was very active in the LGBTQ community, even co-founding a student organization to support and advocate for others in his community. "So, for me, just especially in that space [of the graduation], creating a, what I would say would read as a gay presence, a queer presence was really important. And as a secondary thought, it was also, 'Oh, this is really practical. My parents will absolutely be able to see me in this sea of 400 people."

In selecting the flowers, he considered both aesthetics and durability: "I decided it would be really pretty. I wanted a pretty mortarboard. . . . So, I went to the flower mart in downtown Los Angeles. And I wanted to pick flowers that I knew would be sturdy and were able to withstand, you know, hours of not having water and they wouldn't wilt. So I picked chrysanthemums." Working with flowers was not new to Ray:

> I love flowers. I've always had vases of flowers in my house. I garden and grow them . . . I'm thinking of where I lived at the time and the house and the people, and we had had a lot of parties, and I always used flowers for decorations for them . . . instead of having papel picado hanging as a decoration or streamers, what I would do is create little bouquets of flowers and tie them on a long string so . . . instead of having a streamer looping down and up across a room, I had a long string with bouquets of flowers tied [on it].

Once he purchased the chrysanthemums, he configured them into a bouquet and affixed them to his mortarboard: "I was thinking Frida Kahlo-ish, a little Carmen Miranda. I wanted something big, you know?"

He further explained that visibility, especially as a gay man, was important to him:

> When they called my name, I stood up and sashayed across the stage, and waved my flag and turned and bowed to everybody. And so, there I was. I'm like, I've paid a lot of money to go to this school. I'm gonna make a moment out of this. . . . [Wearing the flowers on my cap] was about signaling for me: my gayness, my queerness, femininity. And I love the word 'faggotry' because to me, it's about pageantry. It's about, you know, it's not a negative. It doesn't have a negative connotation to me. It kind of speaks to a performativity. . . . In that way it embodies that, I want to own that because my whole life, I was bullied at school, picked on and singled out. So, for me, it was reclamation of that, you know? And just, yes, I'm going to embody my faggotry and I'm gonna love it. I'm gonna live it and I'm gonna make it something beautiful on my own in any way I can, and this is one of the ways for me that I did that. Because I was certainly the only guy with flowers on his mortarboard.

He described how later on, people shared with him how striking it was "to see somebody that out and gay, and really proud of who they were." "And to me," he continued,

> that's also part of why I did it . . . I rarely got to see other gay people, particularly as a young person. So I just always carried that with me when I came out. Like, I knew how important it was for all the people who were closeted and not able yet to come out, to be able to see other gay people . . . and I knew that would be a big day. There's gonna be kids and families here and, you know, to me, it's pushing against the grain of, oh, that's a day to be, quote/unquote, "more respectable," more quiet. And I'm like, "Hell, no! No!" Because I'm thinking of that little 10-year-old gay kid back there, and other people are like, "Hey, that boy has flowers on his head. What's going on there?" . . . So, I've always tried to be mindful of that, just being out in the world.

His choice to be "out" in college, to not hide his identity as a gay man, created challenges for him. "The student body," he told me, "is coming from the same homophobic society as everyone else, so there are a lot of homophobic people who are not embarrassed to act out their homophobia and their ignorance." When he walked down the hall in his dorm holding his boyfriend's hand, for example, other students tried reporting him to the resident assistant. He explained how that incident was rather mild by comparison to others: "It was anything from that to outright shouting matches to post-its left on my door with death threats . . . I had so many violent incidents happen when I lived in the dorms."

In light of these experiences as a student, Ray further reflected on the different audiences he had in mind as he designed and decorated his mortarboard:

> Yeah, definitely [I decorated it] for myself because, like I said, this is my day. I'm walking across that stage. I've paid a lot to go to school at that school. I had a lot of challenging experiences there around my identity, so it was just really important to own that. And then, yeah, for my community of friends who were there who want to see, you know, I'm an out and proud gay man, queer man, and I wanted to represent that. And again, certainly for the practicality of my family. And yeah, to show the community at large that would be present, we're here, you know, I'm here. I'm walking across the stage with your kids. And I'm proud of who I am . . . because again, I always think that there are LGBT people everywhere, whether they are out or not, and visibility matters.

VISIBILITY MATTERS

The desire for visibility is a key factor driving people's choices to decorate their caps in the first place. The desire to stand out in the crowd, the desire to make the self visibly present in the sea of uniform dress whose purpose is to diminish individuality, the desire to make visible those aspects of the self that were not easily or comfortably expressed in other domains of university life—these ideas came up again and again in my interviews with graduates. Of course, as the examples presented throughout this chapter illustrate, visibility often carries risks, risks that are managed at the level of performance. Putting one's "self" on display opens an individual up to evaluation. These modes of evaluation are not only shaped by what is deemed appropriate by university administrators, fellow graduates, and one's family and friends. They are also shaped by broader social and political contexts, contexts that are often shifting. Brenda (introduced in Vignette #1), for example, felt it to be much more risky to mark herself as undocumented when she graduated with her bachelor's degree in 2017 than when she graduated with her associate's degree two years earlier. The shift in presidential rhetoric she described, and the shift in public discourse about undocumented immigrants that followed, informed the design of her cap in very real ways. She did not forego visibility altogether, featuring the

Spanish language and images of butterflies, a prominent symbol of immigrant rights activism, but her performance of self was shaped in dialogue with these broader contexts.

For Ray (introduced in Vignette #10), his desire for visibility was shaped in part by the risks of visibility he encountered throughout his college experience—and people's responses to his choice not to live as a closeted gay man. Taking an approach of hypervisibility in his mortarboard design, he affixed flowers to his cap in order to reference Frida Kahlo and Carmen Miranda, Latin American women who famously wore flowers on their heads, very aware that he would likely be the only man with flowers on his cap. Drawing on familiar associations carried by the generalized public audience he imagined for his cap—the "indefinite concretized other" (Bakhtin et al. 1986, 95)—he sought to invoke meanings of femininity and strength to mark himself as openly and proudly queer in the space of commencement.

Both Ray and Isabel (introduced in Vignette #9) gave voice to their hope that others—the "little 10-year-old gay kid," people who have experienced mental health struggles and suicidal thoughts—would see themselves in the performances of self, put on display on their caps, and find comfort and affirmation in that point of connection. For each of them, decorating their mortarboards was not just an act of self-expression; it was an act of destigmatization.

To reiterate Ray's words, "visibility matters." The very act of putting oneself on display, purposefully making oneself visible by wearing a personalized mortarboard, is enacted in dialogue with both intimate social contexts and broader sociopolitical contexts, carrying meanings that are both personal and larger than personal. The following two chapters will turn more focused attention to this interplay between the personal and the political, first within the ritual space of the commencement ceremony itself and then on social media platforms as decorated caps are re-presented in new contexts of public display.

3

Dress and the Visual Rhetorics of Belonging and Exclusion in the Commencement Ritual

WHILE THE PREVIOUS CHAPTER FOCUSED attention on the individuals who adorned their heads with decorated mortarboards, highlighting the often complex personal and performative decision-making processes informing these individual acts of display, this chapter pans out to examine more closely the primary context of display and interpretive frame for these personal performances, specifically the commencement ceremony and the visual rhetorics of belonging and exclusion embedded within it.

During my conversation with Ray, the graduate introduced in chapter 2 (Vignette #10) who adorned his cap with real flowers and carried a rainbow flag as he "sashayed across the stage" during his graduation ceremony in 1999, he explained that, as a first-generation Chicano student coming from a working-class background, "this [the university] was not my world." Drawing connections to his experiences as a queer person of color, he elaborated on this point: "I'm very aware how hostile the world is to me, and including institutions that I have to participate in that, again, have this sense of prestige. I know I'm not the student that that school had in mind."

Ray's words here highlight ideas that emerged often in my conversations with graduates, particularly individuals of marginalized identities—namely, that the university was not a space where they felt comfortable, where they easily belonged.[1] For Ray, the choices he made in what he wore and how he moved in the highly ritualized spectacle of graduation served as an intervention of sorts, what Louis M. Maraj (2020) calls a *rhetorical reclamation*: "For me," Ray asserted, "it was about bringing my full self and owning that space."[2]

https://doi.org/10.7330/9781646425259.c003

As a ritual, the commencement ceremony functions not only as a rite of passage—performatively marking the transition of individual graduates from one stage of life to another—but also as a rite of intensification that affirms institutional narratives about the purpose and value of education. A highly formalized and scripted event, its different components—layout of the physical space, conventions for how to move one's body in that space, designated roles for different participants, and ceremonial costume, among others—all work together to formally and symbolically perform the core values of the institution (Manning 2000; Magolda 2003).

In each interview I conducted, I asked individuals whether they saw their personalized mortarboard as fitting in with the goals of the commencement ceremony. Strikingly, almost all of the white individuals said that they did. Experiencing commencement as a space of celebration, these individuals saw their personalized acts of expression as making the event more personally meaningful and, by extension, strengthening its celebratory goals. Graduates who identified as people of color, while also recognizing commencement as an important moment of celebration, were more likely to talk about wearing a decorated mortarboard—visibly bringing their "self" into the ritual space of commencement—as pushing back against the goals of the ceremony and by extension the core values of the institution.

Recognizing that the commencement ceremony functions as a space for the reassertion of institutional norms, it is not necessarily surprising how different types of students brought different interpretations to the act of displaying their decorated mortarboards in this space. As is well-documented in the scholarship of higher education, the campus environments in many educational institutions are built around "structures and practices that reflect assumptions that preserve predominantly White norms" (Hurtado and Ponjuan 2005, 235). While whiteness is typically invisible, unmarked (at least to those who hold more privileged positions), it nevertheless remains central to the somatic norms (Puwar 2004), and in turn the day-to-day institutional norms, that work to mark bodies that deviate from that norm. As Sara Ahmed tells us, "bodies stick out when they are out of place" (Ahmed 2012, 41), so that just by not fulfilling the implied expectation of whiteness, one's body can cause discomfort when "whiteness is what the institution is oriented around" (Ahmed 2012, 41). In what follows, I consider more fully how the embodied rhetorics of commencement ceremonies work to reinforce dynamics of (in)visibility and exclusion prevalent in campus cultures more broadly.

THE ROLE OF DRESS IN THE RITUAL OF COMMENCEMENT

Academic dress plays a central role in the ritual of commencement. Indeed, the standardized mortarboard and academic robe (popularly referred to as the cap and gown) have become widely recognizable symbols of academia in general and academic accomplishments in particular. The now traditional academic dress in the United States has its origins in twelfth- and thirteenth-century Europe, where monks and priests wore long, flowing robes with loose-fitting sleeves (Hargreaves-Mawdsley 1978). "Prior to the organization of European universities," R. Eric Platt and Lauren Huffman Walker explain in the article "Regalia Remembered," "monasteries and abbeys were the centers of Western knowledge and learning. . . . When monastic education passed into the age of British universities, clerical gowns were retained for symbolic purposes as they represented academic rigor and the studious life" (Platt and Walker 2019, 129).

The mortarboard, the four-sided hat that is such a recognizable component of American academic dress in the present day, grew out of fifteenth-century hat fashions in Italy (Hargreaves-Mawdsley 1978), though it became especially popular in England in the seventeenth century. Initially adopted by Oxford University, which is why the mortarboard is also known as the Oxford cap, it drew on the emancipatory meanings of headwear in the laws of ancient Rome, where the ability to wear a cap or head covering marked a slave's freedom. Integrating this meaning into academic dress, Oxford University adorned the heads of Master of Arts graduates with a cap to signal "emancipation from bachelorhood" (Walters 1939, 4; cited in Platt and Walker 2019, 131).

The European styles of academic dress were adopted in educational institutions in the United States, an adoption that began to be standardized with intent in the late nineteenth century. In 1895, an Intercollegiate Commission created the first set of American commencement regalia standards. Put forth "as strong recommendations rather than strictly enforced rules" (Platt and Walker 2019, 131), they were subsequently adopted by institutions including Brown University, Hampden-Sydney College, the University of Chicago, and Yale University (Leonard 2010). These recommended standards were further codified by the Academic Council on Education (or the ACE) in 1932. By the mid-twentieth century, most institutions of higher education (and increasingly high schools) followed the ACE guidelines.

This standardization of academic dress, particularly in the heightened ritual context of commencement, serves several different functions. On the one hand, it visually marks distinctions in academic accomplishments, creating a "hierarchy of robe design" (Bronner 2012, 390). While highlighting certain distinctions in the academic domain, it also works (by design) to erase others. In reference to the standardization efforts in the late nineteenth and early twentieth centuries, Platt and Walker explain that "US colleges and universities desired to create a standard of academic dress that promoted the American ideal of equality and opportunity for all scholars." David T. Boven elaborates, explaining how

> the wealthy trust-fund students graduating from an American university would dress the same as a scholarship student with only one suit. Because they were equals in academic terms, they would also be equal in their vesture. (Boven 2009, 168; cited in Platt and Walker 2019, 131)

This coincided with larger shifts in public understandings—and political framings—of the purpose of higher education. As Simon Bronner explains: "Whereas the public expected colleges in the nineteenth century to be exclusive from their social surroundings, commentators fueled by Progressive Era reform increasingly called upon schools to represent the look of society and take action to improve it" (Bronner 2012, 19).

In the present day, through the heightened symbolism of the cap and gown, donning academic dress allows graduates to celebrate their individual academic accomplishments while also fostering a sense of community both with their fellow graduates and with those who graduated before them (Platt and Walker 2019, 137). Adorning oneself in a costume with historical roots visibly positions the graduate within a longer legacy of education, a legacy that has its roots in medieval Europe.

This use of dress to visibly mark individuals as part of communities across space and time is inspiring to many graduates, adding a kind of weight, or gravitas, to the celebratory moment of individual accomplishment. Of course, as will become clear below, such public performances of *community* often do the work of drawing boundaries and articulating the limits of inclusion—implicitly or explicitly designating who belongs in the vision of community and who does not.

NATIVE DRESS AT GRADUATION: MARKING AND MANAGING DIFFERENCE

These dynamics are especially visible in recurring conflicts between school districts whose policies do not allow for any modifications to the standard cap and gown and Native American graduates wishing to wear traditional regalia for their graduation ceremonies. Most often, these conflicts have arisen around whether or not Native American graduates are allowed to wear an eagle feather, an act that carries great cultural and religious significance, on their mortarboards. Conflicts have also arisen over graduates wishing to adorn their caps with beading.

In these cases of conflict, the language used to justify the bans typically falls within overlapping categories. The first category highlights the importance of preserving the formality of the ceremony, minimizing "disruption" or "distractions" and "maintaining a dignified atmosphere." The importance of formality is articulated in terms of binaries such as serious versus frivolous and appropriate versus inappropriate, often leading to a "slippery slope" argument, as expressed in one case by a Montana state senator who, citing a hypothetical situation where a student might want to wear a headdress, said: "The graduation is a big ceremony. It's an important thing. . . . At what point do you get where it's really out there, you say, from a cap and gown?" (Hoffman 2017).

Another common category of justification focuses on the importance of preserving uniformity—that is, diminishing the differences between graduates in order to highlight what they have in common—with the ultimate goal of equally celebrating the class as a whole. According to one school district's spokeswoman, the purpose of banning nonacademic accessories during the ceremony is "to maintain uniformity across the graduating class" (Reuters 2015). Uniformity is often discussed with the language of neutrality, as school spokespersons use the terminology of "content neutral standards" and emphasize that the bans include wearing stoles, leis, and religious necklaces, so that Native American students are not the only ones who are restricted from modifying the graduation dress.

This notion of neutrality has been central to how these cases have been framed within the legal domain. Consider, for example, the court ruling for the 2015 case of *Hayden Griffith v. Caney Valley Public School District*, which found in favor of the school district. It reads:

> Neutral rules of general applicability normally do not raise free exercise concerns even if they incidentally burden a particular religious practice or belief. *Id.* (citing *Employment Div. v. Smith*, 494 U.S. 872, 879, 110 S.Ct. 1595, 108 L.Ed.2d 876 [1990])
>
> The undersigned finds that the School's policy of prohibiting any decoration of graduation caps is a neutral policy of general applicability and therefore it need only be rationally related to a legitimate school interest to survive Plaintiff's challenge. (Fort 2015)

This argument invokes the modernist ideal of rationality and frames neutrality as a kind of equal opportunity exclusion, so that even if it burdens a particular religious practice or belief, it does so "incidentally." Of course, as is well-documented in fields including folklore studies, disability studies, and critical whiteness studies, among others, rhetoric of neutrality constructs categories of the "unmarked," categories that carry great rhetorical power because they are seen as untainted and natural.

While less common, another rationale presented for these bans identifies the importance of preserving traditions, as we see articulated in the words of one high school principal: "It wasn't any kind of prejudice. It was about keeping on tradition" (Calvan 2017).[3] This framing of the issue notably mirrors invocations of *tradition* often used to defend and claim legitimacy for other practices that many Native Americans have recognized as problematic—for example, the numerous cases of school or team mascots that portray racially and culturally insensitive stereotypes, such as Chief Wahoo of the Cleveland Indians baseball team or Chief Illinewick of the University of Illinois (cf. Schmitt 2013). In the latter scenarios, where critics have vocally taken issue with misinformed and caricatured representations of Native American people and cultures, appeals to *tradition*—and the authority the term invokes—are similarly used to dismiss the concerns raised by Native voices.

Those who oppose these bans have employed counterarguments that seek to destabilize some of the core assumptions guiding the rhetoric used to justify them. Many, for example, highlight that wearing an eagle feather is a sacred act connected with significant milestones in an individual's life, so that wearing it during the ceremony does not take away from the formality and sanctity (and thus the *value*) of the occasion—it adds to it. In a 2015 letter urging one school district to revise its "no adornment" policy, Melvin Monette, the president of the National Indian Education Association, explained: "Eagle feathers are religious, cultural symbols and are worn with great care and respect. Native students adorn the eagle feather during graduation to acknowledge the accomplishment and moving towards the next path in the student's life" (Monette 2015).

Attorneys working to fight a similar ban implemented in a different school district further explained the ritual significance of the eagle feather:

> Typically, an eagle feather is given only in times of great honor—for example, eagle feathers are given to mark great personal achievement. The gift of an eagle feather to a youth is a great honor and is typically given to recognize an important transition in his or her life. Many young people are given eagle feathers upon graduation from high school to signify

achievement of this important educational journey and the honor the graduate brings to his or her family, community, and tribe. (Fort 2014)

Similar counterarguments are employed when addressing the significance of wearing a beaded cap. In spring 2019, for example, the ACLU wrote the following in a letter on behalf of a Native American student in Arizona who sought to protest her school's graduation dress policy: "The beadwork prepared by Ms. Waln's father for her graduation cap has important religious meaning: It signifies and honors the spiritual role that family plays in the graduate's success" (Longhi 2019).

Another graduate who wanted to wear a beaded cap explained: "It is not decoration, to flaunt. In any ceremony, it's part of us as Natives" (Schorchit 2017).[4] Others pointed out that if visual uniformity was the goal, so that the class as a whole could be celebrated, it was already disrupted by the presence of the highly visible honor cords. Still others highlighted the importance of appreciating difference and diversity, directly quoting from school mission statements to foreground how these values are already espoused in, and thus in line with, the stated goals of educational institutions.

For example, Kylie Oversen, a member of the North Dakota House of Representatives, wrote the following in a letter urging one school district to reverse the ban:

Supporting Native American students' decision to wear an eagle feather during a graduation ceremony falls in line with the philosophy of Grand Forks Central High School, which states the programs of the school will "encourage students to develop responsibility to self and to others and to understand the benefits of cultural diversity to their intellectual, physical, economic, cultural, or religious differences." It is evident to me, wearing of the eagle feather would promote cultural understanding and would ensure equal rights for our Native American students. (Oversen 2014)

Articulating the importance of visibly valuing diversity not only for Native American students, but for the general community more broadly, a self-identified white alumnus wrote:

Cultural diversity is incredibly important in our increasingly global society. To fully and adequately equip all of our students for the 21st century economy, it is imperative that they are exposed to other cultures. Moreover, it is essential that leaders model respect and inclusion. This is particularly pertinent in North Dakota where we have a rather homogenous population and fewer opportunities to experience other cultures and perspectives. (Schaefer 2015)

In response to pushback against the bans from Native American students, their families, and community members, some schools and districts have ultimately reversed their policies, though others have offered compromises, including:

- Allowing students to wear the eagle feather during some parts of the ceremony but not others
- Allowing students to carry the feather or wear it in their hair or on a necklace, but not attached to the cap
- Having students carry the eagle feather under the robe during the ceremony (particularly when the graduate was walking across the stage) and then taking it out after the official ceremony was over
- In the cases of beaded caps, requiring graduates to purchase two caps—a plain one to wear during the ceremony and a second one that could be decorated and worn for photographs

Central to all of these offers is an attempt at managing difference, extracting it from the key symbol of the event (the mortarboard), separating it out from the pinnacle moment of the commencement ritual (walking across the stage to receive the diploma), or allowing it to be present but requiring that it not be visible. Indeed, the desire to manage the visibility of marked difference within the visual rhetorics of the commencement is readily apparent in the language justifying the bans. Consider the wording below in the Magistrate Judges' 2015 decision in *Griffith v. Caney Valley Public Schools*:

> The School demonstrated that the graduation ceremony is a formal ceremony and that the unity of the graduating class as a whole is fostered by *the uniformity of the caps which are the most prominently visible part of the graduation regalia viewed by the audience to the graduation.* Prohibiting decoration of any graduation cap by any student for any purpose serves these legitimate interests. Based on the application of these established principles the undersigned finds that Plaintiff has not demonstrated a substantial likelihood of success on her First Amendment Free Exercise of Religion claim. (Fort 2015, emphasis added)

Equally clear are the power dynamics embedded in these conflicts, for as Alison Dundes Renteln reminds us in her discussion of dress codes, "It must be noted at the outset that as ethnic minorities are usually in positions of relative powerlessness, they themselves rarely determine dress codes. Consequently, they do not decide what the 'image' of the establishment or institution should be" (Dundes Renteln 2004, 260). Indeed, at both the individual and the collective level, these cases of prohibiting the integration of Native American regalia into the space of the commencement ritual illustrate "the presumption of assimilation," referring specifically to the ethnocentrism pervading institutions in the United States, including its legal and educational systems, embodied in the attitude "that individuals from other cultures should conform to a single national standard" (Dundes Renteln 2004, 15).

In defending the students' rights to make visible their Native American identities in the ritual space of commencement, many identify these bans as an active form of erasure, erasure that has very real historical precedents. As one student explained to *Indian Country Today Media Network*, "They said I have to have it inside my gown, and I could only have it out afterwards. So I could not have it when I was going out on stage. . . . It makes me feel like I have to hide who I am" (Gutierrez 2016). In the words of another student reported by the *Arizona Republic*, "why do I have to cover up my culture underneath a gown?" "It's disappointing that there's still this kind of suppression at a school that teaches us to learn from history" (Longhi 2019).

Others drew connections to "the boarding school era" in the United States and elsewhere, where indigenous youth were taken away from their families and sent to boarding schools for the purpose of stripping them of their culture, religion, and language—a purpose famously summed up with the phrase "kill the Indian . . . and save the man."[5] The body, notably, was the site of much of this work, as children were forced to wear uniforms and cut their hair. Zoey Serebriany, a blogger for the Lakota People's Law Project, wrote that "preventing students from wearing regalia at graduation is a continuation of the aggressive assimilation policy that the US has inflicted on Native people for much of the last two centuries" (Serebriany 2019). In the words of another blogger, Heather Torres, "school districts recycle assimilationist values in their graduation attire policies by viewing tribal regalia as informal, inappropriate, and undignified" (Torres 2016).

Others foreground how the erasure and marginalization of Native American peoples in the United States continues on into the present, citing, for example, curricula presenting colonized versions of history and the higher-than-average attrition rates of Native American students, which makes the visibility of Native regalia at graduation ceremonies all the more important. In the words of Mary Levi of the National Education Association American Indian/Alaska Native Caucus, "bring up eagle feathers for graduation, and you're told you're just remembering the past. But it's very present. The reason why these students need to represent their cultures is to show others and themselves that they are still here today" (Schorchit 2017).

In 2015, SaNoah LaRocque and Bettyanne Thomas, two Native American students in Grand Forks, North Dakota, initiated the hashtag #LetTheFeathersFly to raise the visibility of their campaign to change their school district's policy banning Native regalia at graduation. The hashtag subsequently marked a growing movement of framing Native visibility as both visual sovereignty (Raheja 2011) and resistance, amplifying the visibility of Native Americans claiming space in educational institutions and the broader contexts of inequality that make this visibility necessary. One tweet, for example, asserts: "The forced assimilation continues today," accompanied by the hashtags #LetTheFeathersFly, #NativeLivesMatter, and #ResistCulturalGenocide (Native Lives Matter 2015). Another tweet, accompanied by an image of the backs of several graduates sitting in rows wearing mortarboards adorned with beading, reads: "'This photo of my daughter's high school graduation makes my heart happy. In a world where they tried to make Native Americans extinct, we survived and are climbing the ladders to success and bringing our culture with us'–Dawn Begay #LetTheFeathersFly" (Eldridge 2019).

Others defending the rights of Native American students to wear regalia during graduation ceremonies focus on the hypocrisy of institutions that purport to value cultural differences but only "allow" the display of difference in limited spaces and times. One mother identified other school-sponsored enactments of community that are by no means unifying, especially for Native American students and community members, raising the implicit question of why displays of so-called native culture are allowed in one space but not the other: "I've sat at football games for the four years that [my son] spent there," she said. "And I've watched them mock Native Americans. And I've watched them use hand drums. And I've sat there, and I've stayed quiet, and I've stayed respectful, even when it goes against my own beliefs—that I am not a mascot, and neither are my ancestors. But [graduation] was [my son's] day, so that's where I stand" (Ouellet 2017).

Bringing attention to the boundaries containing permissible "difference," one Native American student explained: "They allow us to express our culture during Native American heritage month. . . . But when we want to celebrate our culture and tradition, we're not allowed to, for our last moment as a Skyview senior or a West senior" (Hoffman 2017).

It is the widely recognized social and cultural significance of the commencement ritual in the United States that makes it such a fraught site for these different articulations of what is marked as central, and what is marked as extraneous, to the community image that is visually put on display. As the ongoing conflicts over the proper place of native regalia in this ritual make clear, the visual rhetorics of commencement actively work to mark difference as divergence, making it hypervisible—and as Amy Shuman and Carol Bohmer remind us, "stigma works by assigning, legitimating, and disputing value, and it depends on making things visible, hypervisible or invisible and then naturalizing those positions" (Shuman and Bohmer 2016, 108).[6] Commencement ceremonies are highly symbolic events that reinforce institutional values that, in turn, converge with a dominant national narrative that equates assimilation, or active attempts to render difference invisible, with being a "good" citizen in a pluralistic democratic society.[7] And within this context, when educational institutions try to define the terms of "acceptable" difference and manage its expression, or visibility, the tensions that arise have detrimental effects on those marked as "out of place,"[8] groups that have historically been marginalized in both educational institutions and US culture.

WHO FITS IN THIS SPACE? A POLITICS OF VISIBILITY IN THE RITUAL SPACE OF COMMENCEMENT

While the discussion thus far has focused on cases where the conflicts between educational institutions and members of marginalized groups have been explicit, it is important to recognize that these tensions play out more implicitly as well. It is well-documented, for example, that Black hairstyles, such as afros and braids, have often been deemed inappropriate, unprofessional, and excessive in educational settings—or to use the language of one public school's dress code policy: "extreme," "distracting," "attention-getting."[9] While such dress codes claim to prioritize uniformity, for Black students, columnist Andre Perry (2019) writes, "uniformity too often translates to conformity—to whiteness."[10] To use Shuman and Bohmer's terminology, dress codes construct certain embodied identities as hypervisible, and this hypervisibility that marks these embodiments as outside the norm is part of a larger stigmatizing process of "recognition, misrecognition, estrangement, and othering" (Shuman and Bohmer 2016, 91).[11] In my research for this book, I have not encountered cases where certain types of hairstyles are explicitly banned in the context of commencement ceremonies in particular, but I *have* nevertheless observed a recognition of the ever-present and ongoing dynamics of belonging and exclusion, and cultural pride and erasure, structuring individuals' participation in these events—one that plays out in relation to the hypervisibility of Black hair. One example I encountered online that explicitly engages with these issues features an image of a young Black man with a mortarboard placed atop his afro, along with the caption: "Graduation caps aren't very afro friendly, amirite?"

Each graduation season brings a high circulation of YouTube tutorials and online articles on social media with titles like "How to Wear a Graduation Cap with an Afro or Big Natural Hair." These focus on strategies for fixing natural Black hair to fit within the cap and (more recently) recommendations for adapting the cap to accommodate the hair. As expressed in a tweet shared by @RawNerfertiti, these tips are "For any kinky/curly haired girl whose cap won't fit because of their hair texture. I swear they design caps for only straight hair" (Skwarecki 2017).

We see here a recognition that certain graduates "fit" more easily into this ritualized dress than others. And this is not the only way that issues of "fit" present themselves—consider, for example, the likelihood of so-called ethnic names being mispronounced or, to present another embodied example, the graduates with larger bodies who must choose whether or not to unzip their robes in order to be able to sit through the ceremony more comfortably (González-Martin 2019; see also Marrun 2018). Uniformity may be the stated goal, but in order for some to take part in the visual performance of community by donning the cap and gown, it involves making changes either to one's physical body or to the academic costume itself. The two are not necessarily compatible. In other words, opting to conform at the level of dress is more easily accessible for some types of bodies than others. Given that the commencement ceremony functions as a ritual affirmation of the core values of the institution, lack of fit in this space often maps onto the perceived lack of fit many students experience during their educational journeys leading up to that moment. Big/kinky/curly hair may not be explicitly banned in the ritual space of commencement, but the attention to hair for many graduates leading up to (and on the day of) the ceremony resonates with previous messaging graduates have received in their educational experiences that certain types of hair (and by extension bodies) do not belong.

I find notable, then, in cases where adorning one's graduation dress *is* allowed, the number of decorated mortarboards worn by Black graduates that feature the very hairstyles that are deemed as "matter out of place" in other institutional spaces—vivid images, and often three-dimensional renderings, of afros, braids, and other traditionally black hairstyles.[12] The "negotiation of visibilities" (Shuman and Bohmer 2016, 108) in relation to hair, not just under but also *on* these caps, warrants our attention, for there is clearly a politics of visibility at play in the graduation ceremony.

Figure 3.1. Attention to hair by many Black graduates, both under and on top of the graduation caps, offers just one example of graduates' engagement with a broader politics of visibility in the space of commencement. Photo credit: Cassie Rosita Patterson for the Folklore Archives for the Center for Folklore Studies at The Ohio State University [GCT(OSU)20171217CP87].

Of course, this politics of visibility in the space of commencement does not just play out in the domain of costume and dress. Consider the University of Florida graduation ceremony that made national news in May 2018 when a white faculty marshal physically removed African American students who were doing a celebratory dance on stage. The university president did issue an apology, acknowledging that the marshal was "inappropriately aggressive in rushing students across the stage," but students and commentators alike took note of the racial dynamics at play, given that *Black* students' dancing bodies were policed while other *white* graduates, including graduates doing backflips and taking selfies, were left alone.

The response in this instance was extreme, though nevertheless indicative of the "implicitly raced" (González-Martin 2019) nature of the commencement ritual, particularly though certainly not exclusively at prestigious and primarily white institutions such as the University of Florida. In her observations during several commencement ceremonies at the University of Texas at Austin of how Latinx students occupy the stage, for example through fraternity step routines, Rachel González-Martin considers how these moments serve as a potent "platform for performing ambivalence toward platitudes of institutional inclusion, and in many cases a refusal of empty adherence to socially recognized respectability politics" (González-Martin 2019). This claiming of space on the stage functions as a reversal of power in that symbolically heightened moment, if only for a short time, by halting the flow of the event, temporarily silencing the list of names being read and the very scripted movements of walking across the stage, shaking hands, and receiving one's diploma (González-Martin 2019).

For graduates who have felt pressure to hide aspects of their identities in their educational journeys, refusing to fit easily within the script of the ceremony and claiming the symbolically heightened spaces of the graduation stage or the top of the mortarboard can be an empowering act, especially when bringing those same identities visibly into the foreground.[13] Indeed, it is the symbolically heightened meaning attached to the graduation ritual and its parts—the ritual dress, the ritualized movements—that makes these acts of disruption so powerful.

FROM VISIBLE PRESENCE TO BROADER CRITIQUE

Within the context of the graduation ritual, people don a cap and gown and cross the stage when they have met the institutionally determined benchmarks of academic success and are deemed by the institution to have earned the shift in status from student to graduate. Esa Syeed explains that when students who have experienced marginalization and misrepresentation in their educational journeys put "their own stamps on their caps—a symbol of achieving the 'American dream' of upward mobility—they are asking not to simply be accepted as devotees of meritocracy," but rather "to be seen and accepted on their own terms" (Syeed 2020, 366). These moments also open up opportunities where the institutions themselves can be called into question. Consider, for example, Briceida, selected by her university as one of the outstanding graduates recognized onstage during the graduation ceremony. A commencement tradition meant to "highlight exceptional students who embody the academic, research, and community impact of the graduating class" (UNLV Media Relations 2017), the recipients of these awards often have very high GPAs, significant awards, academic publications, and plans to attend graduate school—all recognized markers of academic success. As a McNair scholar and recipient of several competitive scholarships with a 3.9 GPA, a peer-reviewed journal publication, impressive leadership experience on campus, and plans to begin a PhD program at a prestigious university the following fall, Briceida clearly fit the criteria for the university's vision of an exceptional student, one who hit the marks

Figure 3.2. Many graduates, particularly graduates who have felt marginalized in the university setting, understand their visible presence in the space of commencement to be an act of resistance. Photo credit: Sheila Bock.

of conventional academic success. When she stood on stage to receive this honor, she wore a mortarboard topped with the words "nosotrxs somos resistencia" (which translates from Spanish to "we are resistance") against a multicolored glittery background. An artificial yellow flower stood in for the first "o" in the word "somos," and the front of the cap featured a brightly colored arrangement of artificial flowers (see figure 3.2).

In the words of Briceida, a queer graduate and child of Mexican immigrants, "For me, students of color, poor students, queer students, marginalized students *are resistance* to these white supremacist heteropatriarchal structures that create and reproduce harm and violence." In other words, the very act of *being present* in an institution of higher education, whether as a student working toward a degree or as a graduate ritually marking that accomplishment, is inherently subversive given the structural inequalities that serve as barriers for many people to even get to that point. Making that presence *visible* on one's cap further challenges the norms that naturalize who fits easily into the space of the institution and who does not. Standing on the stage to be recognized as an exemplar of (academic) student success, the message presented on her cap worked to complicate how she was positioned in that space.

As Briceida's words express, her success comes not *because* of the institution of the university. She has succeeded *despite* the structural inequalities embedded within it, a sentiment shared by many of the people I talked to for this research, including Ray from earlier in this chapter when he noted that "I know I'm not the student that that school had in mind." Responding to these circumstances, many students of color use the blank canvas of the mortarboard to make their experiences of exclusion visible. "'We out' (Harriet Tubman)" read a cap worn by one Black graduate, referencing African Americans' experiences with slavery. A cap worn by another Black graduate was emblazoned with the words "finally got TF out," along with an image of the terrified face of the character Chris Washington from the 2017 horror film *Get Out*, a single tear streaming down his cheek. This cap's design referenced the fictional story of a Black man visiting his white girlfriend's family in a white suburban community that at first appears friendly but reveals itself to be ultimately threatening to Black people. And yet another cap featured an image of the woman from the popular BBQ Becky Internet meme, along with the text: "Hi 911, they out here getting degrees." This design made reference to the widespread and dangerous occurrence—one that is mocked in a variety of memes featuring women dubbed "BBQ Becky," "Permit Patty," and "Karen"—of white women calling the police on Black people engaged in innocuous activities, effectively constructing them as a threat that must be stopped in order to put Black people "in their place."[14] On one level these caps express the graduates' relief at being done with the trials and tribulations of college life, though they simultaneously work to mark the graduates' time as a student in the university as being heavily shaped by hostile racial climates on campus (Hurtado 1992; Pewewardy and Frey 2002; Reid and Radhakrishnan 2003; Serrano 2020). They also make visible the recognition that, despite the achievement of earning a college degree and the potential for financial and social opportunities it opens up, hostile racial climates extend well beyond the bounds of the university and will continue to be a force to be reckoned with.

The visual rhetorics of belonging and inclusion within the commencement ritual, as I hope this chapter makes clear, take shape in dialogue with the social and political discourses of belonging in the United States more broadly. The following chapter engages more explicitly with how graduates position themselves (and are positioned by others) within these broader discourses as decorated mortarboards find new contexts of display on social media.

4

Into the Public Sphere
Countering, Rearticulating, and Reimagining Dominant
Narratives of Citizenship

REFLECTING IN 2017 ON THE INCREASING NUMBER of graduation caps adorned with social justice messages by Latinx graduates within the last couple of years, Brenda (introduced in Vignette #1 in chapter 2) told me:

> They started off as a way to kind of embrace who we are, the struggles that we've gone through and to show like, yes, I've made it. Regardless of what I've gone through, I've made it. But I think now, with everything that's going on [i.e., the heightened anti-immigration rhetoric], I feel like not a lot of people are happy with the way things are going for our country and the [racist and xenophobic] messages our country is embodying. I feel like a lot of people see [decorating their caps with social justice messages] as a way to stand up to that. To have a voice against that. To say, "No, this isn't what America is like. I have different values to what might be going on nationally." And I think it's a way to spread that message. And it's also a way of just letting other people know that you stand with them. That you are one of them.

Brenda's words here illustrate the ways in which, for many, decorating one's mortarboard becomes a way not only to situate oneself as part of a larger community, but to self-consciously use this space to engage with ongoing national debates about belonging and inclusion. Indeed, chapter 3 included multiple examples of graduates using their caps to speak back critically to the values of the university and at the same time recognizing that the university as an institution is a microcosm/reflection of larger structures of inequality.

Commencement ceremonies have often served as spaces for visible political protest. To offer just a handful of examples: The Vietnam War inspired a large number of protests across the United States in the 1960s,

https://doi.org/10.7330/9781646425259.c004

which spilled over into graduation events where students dressed in their caps and gowns carried signs with messages such as "How many will die in Vietnam?" (cf. "Dow Protest at Graduation"). Boston College professors and students held up signs in 2006 that read "not in my name" in protest of speaker Condoleezza Rice, then secretary of state in the George W. Bush administration. When Governor Rick Snyder was the speaker at the Northern Michigan University ceremony in 2018, graduates protested his response to the Flint water crisis by standing up silently and turning their back to him (Seelye 2018). And in 2019, a few UNLV graduates carried a large banner that proclaimed "fuck your wall" in protest of President Donald Trump's immigration policy.

Graduates who adorn their mortarboards with messages of social justice fit within this broader tradition of graduation protest, effectively aligning their caps with the material genre of the protest sign. Higher education is commonly understood to be a key stepping stone in realizing the American dream. Sharing one's political message within the space dedicated to celebrating an important educational milestone *and* integrating it into the ritual costume designed to visually mark that achievement creates a particular interpretive frame for the message on the cap. Specifically, it "authorizes" the individual wearer, so to speak, in their call for attention. Carrying the messages beyond the ceremony itself, social media platforms provide opportunities for new contexts of display that engage with different and more widespread audiences. This chapter considers the interplay between amplified personal performances and collaborative community enactments in these new contexts of display, focusing in particular on the collective presentation of decorated mortarboards marked by the #LatinxGradCaps hashtag.[1]

This hashtag, which began in spring 2016 and has reemerged during subsequent graduation seasons, was initiated by Prisca Dorcas Mojica Rodríguez, founder of Latina Rebels, a social media platform that extends across multiple sites, including Facebook, Instagram, Tumblr, and Twitter. The purpose of Latina Rebels, according to its mission statement, is to empower "fully present Latinidad, one Latina at a time, by disrupting the binary expectations that are placed on Latinas' bodies and minds," and "to f*ck with your colonized expectations of 'acceptability.'"[2] The description on the Facebook page at the time the #LatinxGradCaps hashtag launched in 2016 offers further explanation: "We, as Latinas, are passionate about unveiling the injustices that exist when gender and race (or ethnicity) collide in Latinas' embodied realities. We function to disrupt the 'good' girl versus 'bad' girl binary that is a product of white colonization, which functions to police the bodies and mind of womxn of color—thus by voicing our contextual realities as mostly Latina immigrants, we hope to further the perspective of Latinidad in America."[3]

The #LatinxGradCaps hashtag itself uses the term *Latinx* as an alternative signifier to the *Latina/o* gender binary, similar to how the term *womxn* above works to be more inclusive of a broader range of gender identities.[4] While many of the images posted online with this hashtag feature decorated mortarboards that illustrate more widespread trends I have observed and documented in the tradition more broadly—including, for example, the use of inspirational quotes, popular culture references, expressions of gratitude to parents, and large amounts of flowers and other colorful embellishments to help stand out in the crowd—the feminist activist imperative driving this online community is clearly visible in the mortarboards featured in the posts. Assertions of Latinx feminist identities take many forms, ranging from proclamations like "Soy capaz soy fuerte soy invencible soy mujer" (I am capable I am strong I am invincible I am a woman) to visual and textual references to the Mexican artist and queer feminist icon Frida Kahlo to quotes from the Chicana queer feminist scholar, writer, and activist Gloria Anzaldúa. Working to disrupt the "good girl"/"bad girl" binary, other mortarboards make proud claims to gender-, ethnic-, and class-based identities that often carry negative connotations, such as "educated Chingona" and "you can't spell scholar without chola."[5]

Immigration is also a very prevalent theme in the mortarboards posted with the #LatinxGradCaps. Many posts, for example, make reference to the immigrant status of the graduates or their family members. These references take both visual form in the design of the caps themselves—for example, by including images of butterflies, a prevalent symbol of the immigrant rights movement—and textual form, through phrases like "hija de inmigrantes" (daughter of immigrants), "we migrated so I graduated," and "undocumented unafraid unapologetic." Many of the mortarboards also make explicit reference to the DREAM Act, using the multiple meanings of the word "dream" to situate DREAMers, individuals who arrived in the United States as minors and consequently do not have US citizenship, as belonging within the narrative of the American dream:

> Turning my dreams into reality—undocumented student!
> Dreams without borders gracias Mami y Papá [thank you, Mom and Dad].
> Dreamers can do it too!
> Every dream begins with a dreamer
> Create opportunities NOT walls—1st GEN DREAMer
> American dream

Figure 4.1. Many decorated caps position graduates as DREAMers, individuals who arrived in the United States as minors and consequently do not have US citizenship. Photo credit: Sheila Bock.

The remainder of this chapter will address how the aesthetic and narrative framings of Latinx identities in these online displays individually and collectively work to problematize and reframe prevalent cultural narratives about Latinx individuals, families, and communities, as well as their relationship to the American dream.

PROBLEMATIZING THE AMERICAN DREAM

As noted in the introduction, the ideology of the American dream has been a prevalent force in the history of the United States, emphasizing the core values of freedom, equality of opportunity, and individual rights, along with hard work, perseverance, and an enduring optimism that eventual success is possible (Cullen 2003; Terkel 1980; White 2016). Recognizing the recurring gaps between these ideals and people's lived realities, critiques of the American dream have called attention to the ways in which the concept relies on a conflation between citizenship and whiteness, particularly middle-class whiteness (Dick 2011; Hanson and White 2016; Martínez et al. 2016). Within this framing, assimilation to the white middle-class ideal is a key prerequisite for immigrants to gain access to the dream, a prerequisite that similarly works to exclude people of color from its promises. In the words of Carola and Marcelo Suárez-Orozco, "today's immigrants of color are seen by many as possessing traits that make them 'unmeltable' and incompatible with modern American culture. Like other marginalized groups (such as African Americans and Puerto Ricans), some new immigrants have been characterized as being culturally inferior, lazy, and prone to crime and therefore less deserving of sharing in the dreams of dominant mainstream society" (Suárez-Orozco and Suárez-Orozco 2001, 8). The dominant narrative of migrant "illegality" (Negrón-Gonzales 2014) further exacerbates these negative characterizations.

These mainstream framings construct immigrants of color and their children as standing in the way of others who are considered more deserving of achieving the benefits of the American dream. Anthropologist Leo R. Chavez has looked extensively at how the white-centered framings of the American dream affect Latino immigrants and their US-born counterparts in particular through the construction of what he terms the "Latino threat narrative." "According to the assumptions and taken-for-granted 'truths' inherent in this narrative," Chavez explains, "Latinos are unwilling or incapable of integrating, of becoming part of the national community" (Chavez 2013, 3). This pervasive narrative both homogenizes and pathologizes Latinx communities, framing them as "other" regardless of official citizenship status.

Within this hostile discursive context of marginalization, citizenship is not just a legal site of negotiation but also a cultural one. Expanding the scope of inquiry beyond the legal categories of citizenship, scholars have increasingly turned attention to the idea of cultural citizenship, which refers to "how Latinos are incorporating themselves into US society, while simultaneously developing specifically Latino cultural forms of expression that not only keep identity and heritage alive but significantly enrich the cultural whole of the country" (Flores and Benmayor 1997, 2). Cultural forms of expression, in other words, take on heightened significance and become powerful modes of communication as Latinx individuals and communities navigate the discursive terrain of belonging and exclusion in the United States.

Attending to this discursive terrain of belonging and exclusion, my analysis here takes as its starting point the perspective of what Rachel González-Martin terms Critical Latinx Folkloristics, one that foregrounds "the inter-subjective experiences of people of color in the United States, in particular Latinx communities" by examining "communities and individuals at the interstices between those that are understood as public spheres and those recognized as personal or private spheres" (2020, 431). According to González-Martin, recognizing the interplay between these two domains in the study of expressive culture is crucial for understanding how Latinx individuals and communities create spaces of creative expression within discursive contexts of marginalization and contingent citizenship. Such an approach moves away from prioritizing ethno-nationalist identities (e.g., Mexican American) as modes of orienting people's relationships to the expressive practices under study and instead turns attention to the shared experiences of the Latinidad in the United States and the ways in which cultural expressions create emergent *publics*.

Building upon Michael Warner's understanding of *publics* as being constituted through discourse (Warner 2002), Critical Latinx Folkloristics brings attention to how cultural expressions are shaped by intersectional identities and work as "self-conscious forms of self-documentation that simultaneously refuse outsider judgment to validate the process of public self-creation while also benefitting from legibility to outsider gaze to circulate political dissent" (González-Martin 2020, 447). In short, studying cultural expressions through this lens opens up opportunities to examine not only how people navigate, but also how they actively seek to reorient, dominant discourses of belonging and exclusion.

BEYOND THE COMMENCEMENT RITUAL: THE MEANING(S) OF GRADUATION DRESS IN THE PUBLIC SPHERE

As noted above, attaining an education is widely understood to be one important way of opening up opportunities for achieving the upward mobility promised by the American dream. As a result, academic dress and mortarboards have served as potent symbols used by activists fighting for the Development, Relief, and Education for Alien Minors Act, more commonly known by its acronym the DREAM Act, a legislative proposal providing undocumented immigrants who came to the United States as children with a pathway to citizenship. Immigrant rights activists, for example, have used images of students in graduation robes and mortarboards on T-shirts, posters, and websites to illuminate the contradictory plight of undocumented college students who exemplify the values of hard work and perseverance central to the American dream without having access to the potential rewards due to their circumstances of birth. They have also worn robes and mortarboards in mock graduations at the local and national level, holding banners touting messages such as "now what?" and "it is not my fault my parents brought me here 4 a better future" (Chavez 2013, 187). Indeed, the cap and gown has been viewed as a "battle uniform of the DREAM movement . . . [signifying] the educational achievements of the young (im)migrants and their peers against the odds, their ongoing struggles to obtain degrees, and the centrality of schooling and educational aspirations to the immigrant youth movement" (Seif, Ullman, and Núñez-Mchiri 2014, 172). And as undocumented activists have turned increasingly to digital media and communication technologies "to create new spaces for self-representation and mobilization" (Seif 2011, 71), the imagery of graduation dress continues to feature prominently as activists work to counteract the problematic rhetoric surrounding undocumented immigrants as both individuals and communities.

In spring 2017, for example, UndocuMedia and Define American—a nonprofit media and culture organization that seeks to use the power of storytelling to shift conversations about immigrants and citizenship in the United States—launched the #ImmiGrad hashtag, with the express purpose of "giving immigrants and the children of immigrants a platform to break down harmful stereotypes and to celebrate their accomplishments" (Remezcla Estaff 2017). Many posts tagged with this hashtag, along with the #undocugrad hashtag, which started in 2018, featured decorated mortarboards, and the themes found in these posts overlap greatly with posts marked by the #LatinxGradCaps hashtag. In many cases, multiple hashtags were included in the same post. Within these posts, the widespread familiarity of graduation dress and its positive connotations have worked to make activist messaging legible to broader audiences that extend beyond undocumented individuals and their families, thereby increasing their circulation in the social media landscape.

It is clear that the mortarboard itself serves as more than a blank canvas on which people are presenting their personal and political messages. The mortarboard serves as a potent symbol itself. As a recognizable marker of the achievement it signifies, the mortarboard becomes a visible way to rhetorically claim a sense of value and belonging. Within this rhetorical framing, assertions of Latinx and/or immigrant identities (both through the use of the hashtag and through the way the mortarboards are decorated) become forms of *resistance to* and *rearticulations of* dominant narratives excluding these identities from claims to the benefits of citizenship.

Of course, the reliance on the visual currency of higher education to articulate the value of immigrants and their families creates its own exclusions. One graduate using the #LatinxGradCaps hashtag chose to bring attention to this issue by posting a photo of a mortarboard embellished with the text "#Hyperdocumented #SiSePudo." This text references the idea of *hyperdocumentation*—the effort to collect awards, accolades, and academic degrees to compensate for undocumented status (Chang 2011). Marking herself as hyperdocumented, this graduate is notably using this moment of personal achievement to call into question the perceived links between education and legitimacy and acceptance in the United States that in turn perpetuate the good versus bad immigrant narrative. She is also bringing attention to those who do not have mortarboards to post—those who have not pursued or completed their degrees, those who do not fit within this articulation of value and belonging.

Nevertheless, the majority of the posts marked with the #LatinxGradCaps hashtag do not offer such an ambivalent view of the dominant meanings attached to the mortarboard and the educational achievement it visually signifies. Invoking its connection with success and making this success "defiantly visible" in the public of the digital sphere, they become material performances of "violated expectations where problematic hypervisibility is repackaged as a form of oppositional aesthetics" (González 2019, 20).[6]

COUNTERING DOMINANT NARRATIVES SURROUNDING LATINX COMMUNITIES

In 2016, one graduate posted a photo on Instagram featuring a mortarboard laid on top of an indigenous Mexican blanket. The cap included images of an apple, pencils, and a Mexican flag, along with the text "my DNA is successful 2015." While the meaning of the text might be unclear to someone who happened to see it during a commencement ceremony, the online context created the opportunity to provide some additional context in the form of a caption that read: "This was my cap last year. I wrote that because a chairwoman at SJSU said she wouldn't donate money to the university because 'these little Latinas do not have the DNA to be successful.' I had to prove her wrong!" (Latina Rebels 2016b).

In this case, both the design of the cap and its presentation on social media are responding directly to the widespread prevalence of deficit thinking shaping dominant beliefs about lower academic performance and degree completion rates among Latinx students (Matos 2015; Muñoz and Maldonado 2012; Solorzano and Yosso 2002). Deficit thinking takes different forms, at times focusing on genetic or biological deficits (as the words of the San Jose State University chairwoman illustrate) and at times focusing on cultural or linguistic deficits, attributing low educational attainment to families' lack of assimilation to US values and norms (regardless of legal citizenship status).

Figure 4.2. Mortarboards highlighting dichos such as this one can work to challenge deficit models that situate cultural ways of knowing as being at odds with academic achievement. Photo credit: Brenda Carolina Cruz Gomez.

Scholars of education have challenged such deficit models that situate cultural ways of knowing as being at odds with academic achievement, bringing attention to how students draw on pedagogies of the home (Delgado Bernal 2001) and other cultural assets to help them navigate their schooling experiences, including historias familiares (family stories), dichos (proverbs, popular sayings), and consejos (advice-giving narratives) (Marrun 2020).[7] Notably, these genres feature prominently in many of the posts shared with the #LatinxGradCaps hashtag, emphasizing their importance to the individual graduate's success and publicly countering the cultural deficit thinking that structures dominant narratives about Latinx families and communities more broadly. For example, one post using this hashtag on Instagram shared a photo of a cap on Instagram that proclaimed: "me puse las pilas!" The accompanying caption included an explanation of how the graduate's mother always said this phrase to her when she was growing up, noting how having these words ingrained in her mind helped her keep going and put in the effort when pursuing her college degree.

Family stories of hardship and sacrifice also are a recurring theme in many of these posts, stories that, according to Norma Marrun, foster "a culture of possibility" (Marrun 2020, 173) when told and retold within families, which in turn works to motivate Latinx students to do well in school. Many of the mortarboards feature text that explicitly situates the accomplishment of attaining a college degree as part of an ongoing family immigration story, through phrases like "para mi mami quien fronteras para que yo este aqui" (for my mama, who crossed borders for me to be here) and "sus sacrificios no fueron en vano" (your sacrifices were not in vain). Further illustrating this theme, many of the mortarboards feature names and photographs of family members.

Given Latina Rebels' goals of "voicing our contextual realities as mostly Latina immigrants," many of the posts featuring decorated mortarboards foreground feminine gender identities as key dimensions of graduates' contextual realities. These posts often highlight these identities as key parts of the ongoing family stories being shared, as in the accompanying explanation above, as well as through mortarboards proclaiming, "para las mujeres fuertes en mi familia" (for the strong women in my family), "chingona como mi madre" (badass like my mother), and "here b/c of mujeres chingonas como mi mama" (here because of badass women like my mom).

Within the online context of display, numerous photos feature the graduates standing proudly with family members, and many are accompanied by specific family narratives of hard work and overcoming adversity. To offer one example:

> My parents came to this country back in 1993 from Zacatecas, Mexico to give their future children a better future. It took my father 20 years to get his residency and we are still fighting for my mom. Today I made them proud by walking that stage. I do everything for them and without their help and support I wouldn't have done it alone. Those long hours they worked when I was a child I remember. My father working from different restaurants to my mother busting her ass in 12 hour shifts as a housekeeper and in dry cleaners. It's all for us. Immigrants truly work harder than anyone else and they do it for us! Their children! Gracias mama y papa for todo lo que han hecho por mi y mis hermanos [Thank you, Mom and Dad, for everything you have done for me and my siblings]. (Colón 2017)

Recontextualizing these stories and sayings from the home to more public contexts of display on social media serves as one way of asserting (and indeed, rearticulating) the role that family plays in graduates' academic achievements. Within these contexts of display, individual achievements are presented in a way that extends well beyond the personal.

WHERE THE PERSONAL AND THE POLITICAL CONVERGE

As in the tradition of decorating mortarboards more broadly, many of the #LatinxGradCaps mortarboards tout messages of optimism and opportunity—for example, "y seguiré volando" (and I will continue flying)—that exemplify some of the core values of the American dream. At the same time, the use of Spanish in this example as well as others works also to problematize and resist the assimilation narrative associated with the dream. The prevalence of flag images in these mortarboards, or the colors and imagery associated with specific flags, does similar work.[8] Some of these caps include imagery from both the United States flag and other flags, communicating alignment with different national identities and cultural heritages. A good number, however, notably make visible the graduates' connections to countries of origin only, not just through flag imagery but also through folk speech (e.g., "pura vida" [pure life]).[9]

One image posted with the hashtag features a mortarboard that reads, "I carry resilience en la frenta" (on the forehead), an adaptation of a folk saying—"con el nopal en la frente" (with a cactus on the forehead)—used in reference to people who try to deny their Mexican identity.[10] On Instagram, the photo of this mortarboard is accompanied by a caption that offers some additional context for the experiences and perspectives of the graduate who wore it: "I used to hate my skin tone & I used to hate being 'just Mexican,' but college changed that. I am proud to be Mexican, I am in love with my perfectly imperfect brown skin, but more than anything I am proud of my struggle because it makes this moment mean so much more" (Latina Rebels 2016c).

Struggle and resilience, in fact, are recurring themes in the mortarboard images posted with this hashtag. Several, for example, make textual or visual reference to the phrase "They tried to bury us. They didn't know we were seeds." Originally written by gay Greek poet Dinos Christianopoulos, these words were adopted by the Zapatista movement and have come into common use by Mexican and Mexican American activists, often labeled in online memes as a Mexican proverb. One mortarboard featuring this quote was accompanied by the following caption:

> My papi was on his death bed on April 11, 2015 due to a traumatic brain injury. The doctors told us he had a slim chance. I was angry. Why did I take so long in school? He is supposed to be there to see his little girl receive her bachelor's degree. Here we are a year later and my papi will be in the stands like a seed who has risen with new life. Like all of us, the children of immigrants, la raza . . . we rise against all odds. My papi

Figure 4.3. Integrating flag imagery into the designs of decorated mortarboards is one way graduates position themselves in relation to different national identities and cultural heritages. Photo credit: Sheila Bock.

taught me that. This is political. This is personal. This is all of us. (Latina Rebels 2016a)

This caption exemplifies a key pattern in the body of posts as a whole marked by the hashtag #LatinxGradCaps: the linking of the personal and the political.

This idea is foregrounded in many of the graduation caps themselves through phrases like "¡sí se puede!" (yes, it can be done!) and "¡sí, se pudo!" (yes, I did it!), phrases *both* infused with personal hope and accomplishment *and* connected to the struggle of working-class Latinx communities and the quest for pro-immigrant rights.[11] We also see other explicit references to specific immigrant rights activist movements both visually (e.g., the "migration is beautiful" butterfly) and textually (e.g., "sin papeles sin miedo" [No papers no fear]).

Other graduates posting with the #LatinxGradCaps hashtag feature raised fists, a gestural tradition of political resistance and solidarity with oppressed groups, either in the visual designs of the mortarboards themselves, as emojis in the captions accompanying the images, or in their poses

Figure 4.4. Mortarboard displays such as this one explicitly link the personal and the political. Photo credit: Sheila Bock.

within the photographs shared on social media.[12] In one post featuring a photo of a graduate raising her fist with her back to the camera, showing a mortarboard adorned with Día de Muertos imagery laid over the colors of the Mexican flag, the accompanying caption reads: "Shout out to the white guy who yelled that I was stupid Mexican when I was 8 years old while doing chalk art. I graduate mañana [tomorrow] and you've never been more wrong" (Latina Rebels 2016e). In fact, many of the images posted with the #LatinxGradCaps hashtag are accompanied by personal narratives or references to formative experiences of racism.

Some of the mortarboards posted with the hashtag reference the pervasive narrative that immigrants steal jobs from American-born citizens, proclaiming, "job stealing immigrant" and "TRUCHA, I'm here to steal your job!"[13] Others, particularly when Donald Trump was president, made direct reference to his anti-immigrant rhetoric, as in, "This LATINA TRUMPed the STEREOTYPE," "make America Brown again," "I am one of those people Mexico sent," and "Mexico does send its best." These examples of mortarboard displays, in recontextualizing and reframing Donald Trump's rhetoric, align with Stephany Slaughter's observations that productions of this kind work to construct counternarratives through social media and create ways "to claim discursive spaces for Latinx political perspectives in a media landscape and political process that silence those perspectives" (Slaughter 2016, 543).

Clearly, the posts marked with the #LatinxGradCaps hashtag are shaped in response to the homogenizing and pathologizing dominant narratives circulating about Latinx immigrants and their families. Leo Chavez explains: "How newcomers imagine themselves and are imagined by the larger society in relation to the nation is mediated through the representations of immigrants' lives in media coverage. Media spectacles transform immigrants' lives into virtual lives, which are typically devoid of the nuances and subtleties of real lived lives" (Chavez 2013, 6).

Posts using the #LatinxGradCaps hashtag, particularly those that focus on the experiences of immigration, work actively to problematize mediated representations of Latinx communities and foreground the nuances and subtleties of the real lived lives of the graduates and their families. During an interview with me in 2017, Prisca Dorcas Mojica Rodríguez, the founder of Latina Rebels who initiated the #LatinxGradCaps hashtag, further called attention to the visibility politics grounding people's choices to post with this hashtag, explaining, "I think to be seen is really important for people . . . the 'undocumented and unafraid' movement highlighted that. So . . . being seen and being brown is becoming really important, and it's only going to get more important in . . . these next few years."

Decorating one's mortarboard is an act of personal expression, and the #LatinxGradCaps hashtag works performatively within the digital public sphere to mark the meanings of the decorated mortarboards as *both* personal *and* larger than personal. In other words, these material enactments of creative expression become, to borrow the language of González-Martin, forms of self-documentation that "exist in between autobiography and auto-ethnography, and in this way are neither wholly personal nor wholly communal" (González-Martin 2020, 445).[14]

Material and customary folkloric practices are often indexed in the process of self-documentation, and mortarboards embellished with fresh pupusas, lotería cards, and artwork associated with Día de Muertos take on heightened meaning as "blended symbols of cultural heritage and personal politics" (González-Martin 2020, 439). Popular cultural references do similar work. Mortarboards proclaiming, "he dicho caso cerrado!" (I said, case closed!) and "[graduates in Spanish] 2016," for example, reference Spanish-language television shows and the popular Internet memes they inspired, indexing a humorous shared frame of reference that is marked as distinct from mainstream US culture. Many mortarboards marked with this hashtag also reference Selena Quintanilla Pérez, the Tejana recording artist who posthumously

Figure 4.5. Cultural references ranging from folk traditions to popular culture serve as rich discursive resources, invoking shared community experiences while also disrupting the conflation between assimilation and belonging. Photo credit: Sheila Bock.

became a transnational Latina icon as collective mourning after her untimely death shaped the shifting articulations of Latinidad in the 1990s (Parédez 2009). These references not only demonstrate personal appreciation of her artistry as a musician and performer but also invoke her role as a unifying symbol of "transnational Latin/o American success" (Parédez 2009, 24). The unifying and recognizable force of Selena as symbol can then be instrumentalized in the service of sharing personal sentiments and experiences, as in the case of one mortarboard featuring the text "como la Flor" (like the flower), the title of one of Selena's hit songs, accompanied by this caption:

> it's not what you think; this isn't a tribute to Selena Quintanilla. The lyrics
> do come from one of her greatest hits, if not her greatest hit to ever grace
> the world of music, but this isn't about her. this is about my mom. her
> name is Flor. my mom has always been my greatest motivator, inspiration,
> and hero. Flor defied all the odds. as a single mother who emigrated from
> Mexico, she at times worked two jobs so that she could provide for me
> and my siblings. Flor fought tooth and nail against the world to protect her
> children. Flor has stayed the course and has remained resilient in the face
> of adversity. when you see me know that i come from the ribs of a boss,
> that i'm elevated on the shoulders of a giant, and ready to make today hap-
> pen como la Flor. many doubted Flor and did not believe she could raise
> her kids on her own. well look at us now mom.
>   you did it. I love you. (Latina Rebels 2016d)

This post shares a story that is at once personal and communal, intimate and political. The individual family's immigration story of sacrifice and re-silience resonates with many similar stories attached to this hashtag, and the use of the phrase "como la Flor" in both the design of the mortarboard and the written explanation invokes a shared frame of reference that tran-scends ethno-national identities. Indeed, what draws together the diverse individuals who choose to post images of their decorated mortarboards with the #LatinxGradCaps hashtag is not necessarily shared geographic origins or ethno-national identities but the shared experiences of marginal-ization and contingent citizenship in the United States.

Direct references to recognizable cultural forms and traditions work not only to foreground pride in identity and heritage but also to complicate the conflation of assimilation and belonging. Many of the #LatinxGradCaps exemplify some of the core values associated with the American dream, including optimism and resilience, while at the same time refusing to disen-tangle them from explicitly Latinx identities. Social media platforms further allow individuals to contextualize their caps by sharing individual stories of family hardships and experiences with racism that make visible the conver-gence of the personal and the political in the graduates' lives and direct how the decorated mortarboards (and by extension the meaning of the achieve-ment they signify) should be interpreted by others.

#LATINXGRADCAPS: RE-VALUING, DISRUPTING, AND RE-ENVISIONING THROUGH COLLECTIVE PERFORMANCE

Put on display in social media contexts, the individual performances of activ-ism, solidarity, and resistance to the assimilation narrative within the context of individual ceremonies become *amplified* as they are connected to other, similar types of performances through the hashtag, an aesthetic feature that provides a framework for interpreting individual posts and visibly mark-ing a sense of "groupness" in online performances (Bock 2017).[15] Through this amplification, the collection of posts using the #LatinxGradCaps hashtag makes visible—and indeed constructs—a large and diverse activist community.

Academic dress and mortarboards have served as potent symbols in activists' fights for immigrant rights for decades, and the circulation of posts marked by the #LatinxGradCaps hashtag on social media is carrying on this tradition, as personal experiences encoded into the caps take on meanings of collective political dissent. Take, for example, one image of a decorated mortarboard marked by the hashtag shared by Latina Rebels in March 2017, almost a year after it was initially posted. "My parents crossed the border so I could cross the stage," it reads, and it features a Mexican flag, a United States flag, a monarch butterfly, a red rose, and a graduation gown with a diploma. The accompanying text reads: "White people's president keeps wanting to make us feel like shit. making our parents efforts feel like theft. remind them who we are. and how important our people are, no matter. Love this cap! #latinxgradcaps" (Latina Rebels 2017). In a hostile political climate, the collective performance of personalized mortarboards linked by the #LatinxGradCaps hashtag serves as one such reminder, explicitly valuing the individual, family, and community stories and experiences so often rendered invisible or problematic within broader discourses of the American dream.

Importantly, the analytical lens of Critical Latinx Folkloristics helps us recognize that the posts circulating on social media with the #LatinxGradCaps hashtag are not addressing stable, preexisting communities. For example, the "we" referenced in the post quoted above is not referencing a discrete group of individuals who share ethno-nationalist identities; rather, it is envisioning a diverse and politically active audience with a desire to disrupt the dominant discourses working to devalue and marginalize Latinx communities, an audience with the potential to grow as the post is shared by others via online media and individual reposts. As they do in the caps themselves, the language choices in the captions accompanying the images of the decorated mortarboards (e.g., English only, Spanish only, English and Spanish) also do significant work in envisioning and creating the different publics that form around the visual texts circulating online, both the individual posts and the collection of posts linked together through the hashtag. In short, instead of addressing preexisting communities, the posts marked with the #LatinxGradCaps hashtag are simultaneously imagining and creating emergent publics that question, resist, and reenvision the dynamics of belonging and exclusion embedded in the American dream.

5

Undisciplining Graduation

THIS CHAPTER BRINGS US BACK TO THE DESIGNATED space and time of the commencement ceremony. Spaces of celebration, these are also very disciplined spaces. I draw here on multiple meanings of the term *discipline*—referring both to a branch of knowledge structuring higher education and "the practice of training people to obey rules or a code of behavior" (Oxford Reference). As noted in chapter 3, within this space, participants have clearly scripted and preestablished roles, and there is a hierarchy that is visually marked by differences in dress and one's placement in the physical space. Often, differences are further marked, both visually and spatially, to differentiate the (disciplinary) categories of knowledge and expertise graduates have accumulated during their time at the institution, either by department or college affiliation. And the pathway to moving up in the hierarchy structuring this ritualized space is ostensibly linked to the accumulation of disciplinary knowledge and expertise that is promised by a university education.

The change in status that is ritually marked in the space of commencement also positions graduates within the prevalent and enduring cultural narrative that pursuing higher education is a key stepping stone in achieving the heightened social status and social mobility promised by the American dream, a narrative grounded in what Simon Bronner has described as the "American folk idea of college paving the way to commercial success" (Bronner 2012, 9). While the previous chapter focused on decorated mortarboards' engagement with the American dream within a context of ongoing debates surrounding notions of citizenship (i.e., who belongs and who does not), this chapter turns attention to the more broad-stroke promises embedded in this cultural narrative that links hard work and perseverance with an enduring optimism for eventual success (Cullen 2003; Terkel 1980; White 2016)—and how decorated mortarboards take shape in dialogue with these promises. In the process, this chapter considers how

https://doi.org/10.7330/9781646425259.c005

Figure 5.1. Engaging with themes such as debt and financial hardship, playful mortarboard designs can inspire ambivalent laughter. Photo credit: Sheila Bock.

graduates use their mortarboard displays to position themselves in relation to the conventional cultural narratives of "success" that are performatively reaffirmed within the institutional ritual.

While rituals like commencement are ostensibly "serious" in nature, it should not be surprising to find expressions of humor in this space, expressions juxtaposing the serious and the lighthearted. As Kathleen Manning reminds us, "Using comedy, farce, and cultural faux pas, rituals have the capability to create situations where community members laugh at themselves, make fun of each other, and treat the most serious issues in a manner that pokes fun and creates absurdity" (2000, 9). Consider, for example, the large number of mortarboards calling attention to the excessively high amount of student debt graduates carry now that they have earned their degree. One particularly popular variant of this theme, one I have encountered often, refers to the book and television series *Game of Thrones* by featuring the words, "game of loans—interest is coming." Another cap design that stood out for me (quite literally standing about eight inches tall atop one graduate's mortarboard) displayed a three-dimensional representation of the "I have 3 dollars" meme that was popular at that time (see figure 5.1). The image macro this cap design was based on features the character Patrick Starr from the cartoon *SpongeBob SquarePants* holding up three dollars and expressing his lack of money.

This image macro is often shared online to react to costly scenarios (e.g., "me hanging out with my friends like . . . I have 3 dollars" or "trying to buy the iPhone 6 . . . I have 3 dollars" or "trying to pay for college like . . . I have 3 dollars") ("I Have 3 Dollars" n.d.).

When I have asked graduates donning these types of designs why they decorated their mortarboards the way they did, they have expressed a desire to be funny. The seemingly out-of-place popular culture references work to set up a kind of "play frame," which in turn is meant to elicit laughter from the people who view it. The laughter these caps inspire, though, referencing burdensome debt and financial hardship, is *ambivalent* laughter, laughter that is intertwined with a serious critique of the "value" of the education and the change of social status being celebrated in that moment. Ambivalent laughter is, notably, a key characteristic of the carnivalesque, a notion that emerged out of Mikhail Bakhtin's (1984) work on the writings of Rabelais and has been extended to various sites of festive behavior to call attention to the destabilization of power structures, social transgressions, and irreverence embedded within them. I have seen caps blurring the distinction between the diploma and genitalia, exemplifying another element of the carnivalesque: the mocking of established orders by "thrusting all that society exalts or idealizes [in this case the college degree] downward into the body's 'lower stratum'" (Gabbert and Salud 2009, 213). We might also understand caps that play on the double meaning of BS as standing for "bachelor of science" and "bullshit" (e.g., "Finally done with this BS") to be enacting carnivalesque qualities by invoking scatological imagery at the same time they are trivializing the value of the degree.

In identifying the carnivalesque qualities of some of these cap designs, my goal is not to draw simple parallels to the outrageous, bawdy, and excessive inversion of formal hierarchies that characterized medieval Carnival, or to overassert the disruptive nature of wearing these caps during the commencement ceremony. Just donning the ritual dress of the cap and gown and participating in the formal ceremony, after all, involves reaffirming the institutional and cultural values shaping the collective ritual performance. But if we understand wearing decorated caps as acts of positioning, where individuals situate themselves in relation to broader narratives surrounding higher education in the United States, we might also understand the ambivalence and inversions we see on display in these caps as transforming them into sites of rearticulation, expressive sites that engage in the work of *un*disciplining not only the space of commencement but also the broader cultural narratives that shape it.

Figure 5.2. Graduation caps commonly feature the notion of forward momentum with a clear orientation toward the future. Photo credit: Sheila Bock.

LOOKING AHEAD DOWN THE LINE

Decorated caps often align the individual graduates who wear them with the widely circulating cultural narrative of the American dream, foregrounding its key tenets that also converge with folk ideas central to the US world-view identified by folklorists, including individualism, optimism, unlimited good, and orientation to the future (cf. Dundes 1969, 1971; Toelken 1996). These mortarboards, for example, proclaim messages such as "my future is unlimited," "the best is yet to come," "there's just no telling how far I'll go," "there's a great, big, beautiful tomorrow . . . go live your dream," "on to the next chapter," "PhD bound," "off to medical school," "future OT," and "to be continued . . ." Indeed, this future-oriented worldview is central to the graduation ceremony as a whole, apparent even in the term used to describe it: *commencement*, meaning beginning.

Many caps—such as ones that assert "thank U, next degree" (referencing Ariana Grande's 2019 song "Thank U, Next"), "Now go, and don't look back!" (referencing the 2001 film *Spirited Away*), "keep moving forward," or list degrees in a checklist format—further foreground the notion of forward momentum, along with the sentiment that the degree being celebrated is already old news (see figure 5.2). As Alan Dundes reminds us, within the future orientation found in the US worldview, "The future becomes present immediately and ignominiously into the past" (Dundes 1969, 58–59).

When past experiences are featured on people's caps, they often are framed as obstacles overcome. For example, a graduate named Amy emblazoned her cap with alternating white and gold text that read:

1 EX
2 KIDS
9 JOBS
1 HUSBAND
1 ADDICTION
13 YEARS 127 CREDITS
66K LOANS
=
1 COLLEGE GRAD
!!!

In my interview with Amy, she explained that the primary audience she had in mind for her cap was people she did not know. When I asked what she wanted these people to take away from looking at her cap, she told me:

> I guess there's so many ways you could look at it, but I was hoping that for those non-traditional students . . . a mom who's afraid to go back to school or a student who thought they couldn't get it done in the four years that's typically expected, or whatever their story might be, that there's so many elements here that could have stopped me, but didn't. And I wanted other people to know that whatever their list might be, they could [graduate] if they wanted to anyway.

Similar to the motivations of Isabel (introduced in Vignette #9 in chapter 2), the graduate who chose to foreground her attempted suicide on her cap, we see here how even looking back is done with an eye toward the future as graduates feature past experiences in order to chart a path forward for others who are experiencing similar obstacles.

Foundational to this orientation to the future is the lineal world-view that, according to Alan Dundes, is "so evident in the American definition of success and progress" (1971, 186). The lineal worldview is well-documented in the folk culture of the United States, ranging from common expressions (e.g., "keeping things straight," "getting straight," "staying in line," "toeing the line," being "level-headed," keeping "on the straight and narrow") to vernacular architecture and urban planning to the experience of time and progression through the life course (Dundes 2004; Lee [1959] 1968; Toelken 1996). As Barre Toelken notes in relation to this cultural understanding of time, "the cultural conviction that we move forward on a single line of time has led to a concept of future, the anticipation of future events, and a high evaluation of anything that lies in the future" (1996, 270).

The lineal worldview is apparent in much of college life: the rows of seats structuring classroom spaces; the linear structure of academic essays with an introduction, body, and conclusion (Toelken 1996, 274); the solemn procession of lined-up faculty, administrators, and students at commencement ceremonies; the language of "progression and completion" used by university administrators seeking to streamline students' pathways through degree programs. At UNLV, my own university, the page of the school website dedicated to nontraditional students begins with these words: "The road to a college degree isn't always *a straight line* from start to graduation" ("Non-Traditional Students" n.d., emphasis added). The implication here is that moving forward along a continuous straight line is the norm, the ideal vision against which the very category of nontraditional students takes shape. Those who are able to "keep things straight" in their minds and "stay on track" are the ones most likely to find success "down the line."

THINKING BEYOND THE STRAIGHT AND NARROW

Queer studies scholars have brought attention to the heteronormativity embedded in this view of time—that is, "straight time." In the online documentary *Queer Interruptions*, Evangeline Aguas explains:

> The world seems to function on "straight time"—the life paths and cultural milestones of adolescence, marriage, reproduction, retirement and death. But queer people often stray from that path, being excluded from marriage and child-rearing or experiencing these rituals in a haphazard or disordered way. So queer time is marked by a sense of this disorder: a sense of delay and a stumbling through self-discovery; a rebirth and a resetting of oneself; and a feeling of being out-of-sync with the life trajectories reserved for the more "valuable" and "productive" (heterosexual) members of society. (Aguas 2021)

One of the interviewees in the documentary, Nicole, describes their feelings of "being out-of-sync" in terms of temporal progression in this way:

> I think if I'm comparing myself to folks in my age range then I think I'm, I'm delayed for sure considering that I'm 36 and I'm not finished with my undergrad. Whereas most of my peers are done with their degrees, *been* done, have fam-, have *multiple* kids. I do feel like I am [using air quotes with their fingers] behind in that way. (Aguas 2021)

Nicole's words here gesture toward how lives that don't follow "straight time"—lives not structured around reproduction and other forms of "productivity" for the purpose of accumulating assets to pass on to kin—fall outside of conventional visions of success, the "good" life. It is important to note here that this disconnect between lived experience and "straight time" is not limited to those who identify as queer. For example, sociologist Jennifer M. Silva's interviews with working-class men and women in their twenties and early thirties revealed that

> the transition to adulthood [often] bore little resemblance to the normalized progression of leaving home, completing school, finding a steady job, getting married, and having children that so clearly demarcated the split between childhood and adulthood in the decades following World War II. On the contrary, traditional markers of adulthood haunted them as unattainable, inadequate, or even undesirable, turning coming of age into a journey with no clear destination in sight. (Silva 2012, 511)

Jack Halberstam's work on queer temporalities considers queerness "as an outcome of strange temporalities, imaginative life schedules, and eccentric economic practices" (2005, 12), compelling because of the potential it creates "to open up new life narratives and alternative relations to time and space" (2005, 13). In other words, it generates temporalities that extend beyond *the straight and narrow*. And these queer temporalities certainly informed the design of Nicole's cap when they ultimately graduated. Walking across the stage to receive their diploma, they wore a cap depicting the dismembered body of the Aztec lunar goddess Coyolxauhqui (see figure 5.3). They explained:

> I was introduced to this story from reading Gloria Anzaldúa's posthumous book *Light in the Dark* in a Feminist Research Methods course taught by my mentor Dr. Erika G. Abad. In [this book], Anzaldúa theorized the "Coyolxauhqui Imperative." It is essentially taking the dismembered parts of the self then re-membering and reconstructing these parts to re-create a whole, healed self. When I read this, I instantly thought of fan fiction, the "Bury Your Gays" trope in TV, and I built my Gender & Sexuality Studies capstone project around it. Fan fiction allows readers to re-member dead lesbians from TV shows in universes where queerness does not lead to death. . . . I say that Coyolxauhqui represents my undergraduate experience because of the continuous healing from various things that "tore me apart" over the duration of five years: the break up of a six year relationship (the summer after my 2nd year), intimate partner violence (unrelated to the break up), renegotiating my place in the queer

Figure 5.3. Graduation caps can become sites for reenvisioning the disciplining logics of "straight time." Photo credit: Sheila Bock.

> movement . . . and in higher ed. Whenever I have a breakthrough in ther-
> apy, I'm re-membering the parts of myself that were dismembered from
> trauma in its various forms.

Here their transformation and individual growth are articulated not as a linear progression or as a story of overcoming obstacles through persever-ance but as an ongoing action of re-membering themselves and envisioning alternative possibilities of moving forward—what Halberstam might call "an art of unbecoming" (Halberstam 2011, 88).

This portrayal of re-membering, inspired by the work of writer and scholar of Chicana cultural theory, feminist theory, and queer theory Gloria Anzaldúa, offers a mode of self-presentation that exists outside of the nar-rative of accumulation and forward momentum shaping the commence-ment event as a whole. We might view this cap, then, as a site of visual storytelling that disrupts the (straight) temporalities foundational to the narrative script structuring commencement, a site of rearticulation where the display of self on the mortarboard envisions queer ways of being. In short, we might view Nicole's decorated cap as a site of undisciplining.

Nicole's visual display of re-membering offers one clear illustration of how graduates use decorated mortarboards to reposition themselves in relation to the dominant cultural narratives affirming linearity and forward progression, though this is certainly not the only form of undisciplining I observed during the course of the research for this book. In fact, in some ways this cap was unique as an example of undisciplining, taking shape in conversation with a scholarly text encountered in the college classroom (albeit a scholarly work that transcends disciplinary boundaries). Much more often, these material acts of undisciplining take shape through the recontextualization of seemingly lighter "texts." It is to these seemingly more trivial forms of recontextualization that I will now turn.

UNDISCIPLINING ADULTHOOD

College is often framed as a "coming-of-age transitional period" (Bronner 2012, 377). The commencement ceremony, marking the completion of the college experience, serves to ritually mark this transition to adulthood along the linear path of "straight time." Aligning with this popular understanding of this shift in status, the glittery mortarboard of one UNLV graduate proclaimed, "Welcome to fabulous adulthood," referencing through both text and imagery the iconic "Welcome to fabulous Las Vegas" sign that greets tourists driving into the city and framing adulthood as a destination at which one arrives.

Most often, though, cap designs do not so clearly position adulthood as a stable destination, a definitive shift in status that is clearly in sight. "Yes mom, I have a jacket," one cap says. "Still not ready for the real world, but I'll try to be," says another. And yet another references the 1997 Blink-182 song "Dammit (Growing Up)" in presenting this less-than-confident assertion: "I guess this is growing up."

In using the space of the caps to rearticulate their own position in relation to the larger coming-of-age narrative structuring the event as a whole, individual graduates did not just turn to textual forms of expression; they also turned to children's media. When I first began to pay attention to decorated mortarboards at UNLV's commencement ceremonies, I was struck by the large number of caps featuring characters, words, and imagery from *SpongeBob SquarePants*. This children's show did not air on television until I was just about to graduate from high school, so I had very little knowledge about it. In my (admittedly informal, certainly undisciplined) attempts to understand the appeal of this show among young adults via impromptu conversations and queries on social media, one recurring idea that emerged was the way it offered a feeling of reprieve from the tasks of adulthood, or what in recent years has been termed "adulting."[1] As one twenty-year-old explained: "I liked SpongeBob as a kid because he told good as heck jokes. . . . Now as an adult, I have to watch it just so I can feel like a kid again and not worry about my current responsibilities for like half an hour. . . .

I like the episode where SpongeBob wants to be treated like a baby again because his grandma was treating Patrick like a baby and it stood out because I felt that, man. I lowkey was like, man, I wanna be a baby again, lol."

I also encountered young adults describing how they found a kind of inspiration in the title character, SpongeBob SquarePants, who is described by the fandom website Encyclopedia SpongeBobia as "a fun-loving, hyperactive, clueless, and childish sea sponge with a happy-go-lucky personality" ("SpongeBob SquarePants" n.d.). In the words of one twenty-five-year-old,

> I love that he's a happy character and at the end of the day doesn't give a
> f*** about what people think. I was showing [my husband] some of the
> episodes the other day. I showed him the one where [SpongeBob] wants
> to have muscles like the other guys, so he lies and gets inflatable ones. And
> the one where he tried to be "normal," so he gets a boring 9 to 5 desk job
> and becomes physically smoother and behaves in a duller, boring "adult"
> way. . . . He flips burgers, yet he's so happy. I guess it's all about how you
> see the world.

What we see in both of these reflections on the appeal of *SpongeBob SquarePants*, I'd argue, are critical reflections on the process of becoming a "successful" adult, or rather, what conventional wisdom tells us is required in the ongoing work of *adulting*.

In the book *The Queer Art of Failure* (which, notably for the current discussion, begins with a quote from *SpongeBob SquarePants*), Jack Halberstam identifies "low theory" (adapted from the work of Stuart Hall) and popular knowledge as useful avenues to explore alternatives to conventional notions of success. Rather than merely reevaluating standards of success or the means by which people fall short of them, Halberstam calls upon readers to dismantle the current *logics* of success and failure, foregrounding the question, "What kinds of reward can failure offer us?" (Halberstam 2011, 3). He goes on:

> Perhaps most obviously, failure allows us to escape the punishing norms
> that discipline behavior and manage human development with the goal
> of delivering us from unruly childhoods to orderly and predictable adult-
> hoods. Failure preserves some of the wondrous anarchy of childhood and
> disturbs the supposedly clean boundaries between adults and children, win-
> ners and losers. (Halberstam 2011, 3)

We have already seen examples above of how some of the cap designs work to disrupt the clear-cut boundaries between adulthood and childhood, including through unapologetic references to children's animated shows, a realm of popular culture that, Halberstam asserts, "revel[s] in the domain of failure" (Halberstam 2011, 27), conjuring storyworlds shaped by aspirations that extend beyond "the realms of success and triumph and perfection" (Halberstam 2011, 27). And the connections graduates draw between the storyworlds found in these "low brow" genres and their own life trajectories do more than playfully disrupt, via "silly," "trivial," or "juvenile" visual displays, a ritual ceremony marked by formality, reverence, and the celebration of academic values. I propose that these recontextualizations of media discourse linked to childhood, silliness, and stupidity might also be working to envision alternatives to conventional notions of success, alternatives that allow for the unruly and the disordered. In fact, I'd like to introduce the possibility that these acts of recontextualization in this culturally significant space and time work to "[p]rivilege the naïve or nonsensical" (Halberstam 2011, 12), destabilizing the values of discipline, mastery, and accumulation central to the most recognizable scenarios of success.

POWER, TACTICS, AND CALLING ATTENTION

Indeed, disciplinarity (drawing on Foucault's [1975] work defining it as a technique of modern power) is a central structuring logic to our current system of education. To be taken seriously is a key goal driving the quest for mastery and expertise (and normalization and convention) that structures formal education and the pathways it envisions for the future. As Halberstam reminds us, "The desire to be taken seriously is precisely what compels people to follow the tried and true paths" (Halberstam 2011, 6). But, of course, these tried-and-true paths and disciplined forms of knowledge can and do fall short of their promises—and messages on caps often take note of this. Think back to the decorated cap I introduced at the very beginning of this book that asked, in the wake of Donald Trump's election to the United States presidency, "What does my political science degree mean now?"

I see resonance between this questioning of disciplinary authority via mortarboard, and another cap I observed that showcased an image of Dory, the forgetful fish in the animated Pixar films *Finding Nemo* and *Finding Dory*, and proclaimed, "I already forgot everything." And another with the words "still knows nothing . . ." accompanying an image of the character Jon Snow from *Game of Thrones*, referencing an Internet meme inspired by the quote "You know nothing, Jon Snow." And yet another that read, "what I learned in boating school is . . . ," referencing an Internet meme inspired by a scene in the cartoon *SpongeBob SquarePants*, where the title character

Figure 5.4. Graduation caps often become a tangible space where the tactics of student life are put on display. Photo credit: Sheila Bock.

is unable to complete that sentence when his teacher asks him to, making clear that he has not retained any of the information expected of him (see figure 5.4). An underlying implication in all of these examples is that forgetting disciplined knowledge is not necessarily detrimental. Losing (one's way, one's agenda), after all, creates opportunities to "find another way of making meaning" (Halberstam 2011, 25) and seek alternatives to marking achievement, to craft unexpected pathways to a life well lived.

These last three examples also make visible the *tactical* nature of forgetting. In his study of "the clandestine forms taken by the dispersed, tactical, and makeshift creativity of groups or individuals already caught in the nets of 'discipline'" (de Certeau 1984, xiv–xv), Michel de Certeau identifies tactics as separate from strategies. Strategies, according to de Certeau, stem from subjects of "will and power" and involve the establishment of place that "can be circumscribed as *proper*" (de Certeau 1984, xix, italics in original). Tactics, on the other hand, are fleeting modes of unsettling normalized conventions, a "clever utilization of time" that introduces play into the foundations of power (de Certeau 1984, 39). As participants in the disciplined spaces of education, students employ a range of tactics, "manipulat[ing] the mechanisms of discipline" (de Certeau 1984, xiv) to make these learning spaces "habitable" (cf. Beresin 2015; Henn 2018; Lankshear and Knobel 2002). Offering reading as an illustrative example of tactics, de Certeau brings attention to how acts of reading, the means by which individuals ostensibly come to be informed (i.e., authorized by the logics of power) both inside and outside the formal classroom, are in fact quite "playful, protesting, fugitive" (de Certeau 1984, 175). And acts of forgetting what is deemed significant within systems of education are certainly part of this same process.

Through my research I have encountered many caps that bring attention to student tactics. "Thank you, Google," one cap read (highlighting the role that the nonacademic search engine played in the research this graduate was called to do for class assignments). Another cap, highlighting the tactic of procrastination, featured a ripped piece of lined paper crudely taped onto the top of the mortarboard and extending beyond its edges, disrupting the clean lines of the square-shaped hat. In sloppy handwriting penned with a black marker it read: "Last minute like everything else in college." And yet another proclaimed: "My efficiency is clever laziness."

When such tactics are put on display via the material objects of decorated mortarboards, these expressive acts take on more *strategic* qualities. As Danille Christensen observes in her astute analysis of scrapbooks and feminist zines, these forms

> represent a strategy for challenging norms by demanding attention.
> Because they are material objects, compiled three-dimensional book genres
> are more strategic than less tangible tactics such as reading or listening:
> claiming their own real estate, physical things are more complete victories
> of space over time. As text-artifacts, all compiled book genres extract,
> bound, and present content for display, allowing even the ephemeral to be
> entextualized as evidence by a subject who demonstrates his or her own
> agency in the process. (Christensen 2017, 270)

Similar to the compiled book genres Christensen studied, the decorated mortarboard becomes an opportunity for graduates to "claim their own real estate," and where ephemeral acts that constitute the everyday practices of student life (e.g., forgetting, relying on Google, procrastinating) are entextualized in the physical space of the graduation cap as a means of calling attention to these acts.[2] The setting of display is significant here, too, for commencement is a designated space and time of institutional affirmation, affirming both the value of the institution and its goals as well as the graduate's role as institutional representative. The prescribed cap and gown donned by graduates visually marks this role. Embodying the authority this role confers on the graduates to speak to the value of higher education, many graduates use this space and time to challenge it.

And in this moment of heightened precarity, it is not necessarily surprising that graduates are using their caps in this way. As Anna Lowenhaupt

Figure 5.5. Many decorated mortarboards reference graduates' anxieties and ambivalence about an increasingly precarious future. Photo credit: Sheila Bock.

Tsing suggests in *The Mushroom at the End of the World: On the Possibility of Life in Capitalist Ruins*, "precarity *is* the condition of our time," not the exception to the rule, and "our time is ripe for sensing precarity" (Tsing 2015, 20, emphasis in original). Students "on the ground," so to speak, are very well positioned to see how the educational system is not clearly in alignment with its promises, to find themselves on a well-worn path with no clear outcome. And the caps introduced above highlighting the tactics students use to make institutions of higher education "habitable" present college requirements as procedural rather than generative. "Progress felt great; there was always something better ahead," Tsing writes. "The problem is that progress stopped making sense. More and more of us looked up one day and realized that the emperor had no clothes" (Tsing 2015, 25).[3]

For many, graduation is a time faced with ambivalence. It is a moment where hard work receives celebratory recognition and tangible documentation, bringing hope for a good life ahead. It is also a time when graduates merge their prior notions and expectations with the precarity characterizing our individual and collective futures. And we see these anxieties being articulated in the designs of many decorated caps: "now what . . . ?" "still not ready for the real world," "looking for a sugar mama." One notable cap I encountered indexed the genre of role-playing video games, where the character of the graduate finds himself in a powerless position when facing off with a prospective employer (see figure 5.5). The world that is envisioned here is one where the graduate must be tactical. The structure of the current system leaves very few options.

By way of conclusion, the ritual of commencement is a space where graduates reflect on the value of their educational experiences with an eye toward the future, toward new beginnings. Often, these reflections (at least as they take material and visual form on the decorated caps) diverge from widespread narratives that have both structured and articulated the larger meaning of their educational experiences, meanings that depend on notions of success based simultaneously on discipline, accumulation, and forward momentum. I hope this chapter creates space for understanding these mortarboard displays as sites for rearticulating some key ideas central to the US worldview and envisioning alternatives to these notions of success, alternatives that leave space for decidedly *un*disciplined ways of knowing—the naive, the nonsensical, the unruly, and the liberatory potential of failure.

6

Conclusion
A Brief Reflection on Trivial Matters

IN HIS RICH STUDY OF PERFORMATIVE DISRUPTIONS of popular media texts in folk culture, folklorist Greg Kelley draws historical parallels to the art of illuminating manuscripts—that is, "adding decorative marginalia to scripted texts"—between the twelfth and fourteen centuries (Kelley 2020, 6). "The copyists," Kelley tells us, "were often unruly consumers of the very ecclesiastical texts they produced, and their disruptive point of view found (often humorous) expression in the illuminations themselves" (Kelley 2020, 7). The margins of these religious texts featured images including animals, hybrid beasts, grotesque human figures, and depictions of royalty and clergy. Many also included motifs that "radically destabilized the host text they decorated" (Kelley 2020, 8) through scatological, lustful, and secular themes. Kelley asserts: "These are not just extraneous marginal doodles—as many medieval scholars dismissed them for years. Rather, on the pages of these codices, these illuminations interact in meaningful ways—semiotically and sometimes literally—with the scripted text" (Kelley 2020, 9). They did more than merely embellish the texts; they shaped their meanings.

After completing the research for this book, when I now attend commencement ceremonies, I can't help but see clear parallels between the medieval marginalia Kelley describes and present-day decorated mortarboards in the space of this ritual ceremony. The messages on these caps (be they textual, pictorial, or otherwise) take shape in relation to—and interact with—the relatively stable and consistent scripted "text" of the formal ceremony. Like the marginalia illuminating sacred medieval texts, decorated mortarboards work "to gloss, parody, modernize and problematize the text's authority while never totally undermining it" (Camille 1992, 10; cited in Kelley 2020, 10). And like the images found in the illuminated manuscripts, they have been noticed but nevertheless deemed by many as unimportant.

https://doi.org/10.7330/9781646425259.c006

Figure 6.1. Like the seemingly trivial marginalia in medieval ecclesiastical texts, decorated mortarboards help shape the meaning of the commencement as a whole. Photo credit: Sheila Bock.

In the introduction of this book, I identified one of my key goals as taking mortarboard displays seriously. What inspired my shift from appreciative observer to researcher of this tradition, after all, was the lack of attention these artful, reflexive, and clever expressive forms received in the scholarly literature. Of course, those familiar with the "triviality barrier" (Sutton-Smith 1970) will not be surprised that this rich traditional practice has been overlooked by "serious" scholars. Like children's folklore, housework, and latrinalia—ephemeral forms of expressive culture associated with people (children, housewives) or places (bathrooms) deemed marginal to the *important* aspects of cultural life—decorated mortarboards carry connotations that make them easy to overlook as significant cultural artifacts. Their associations with the ephemeral and the playful are certainly factors that have contributed to their trivialization, not only among academics but also more generally. Often, the crafted designs atop the mortarboards are not meant to endure longer than the time of the ceremony and the post-ceremony pictures. This limited timeframe of significance leads many to overlook them as meaningful forms of expression. Their associations with college students—a group dismissed by many as somehow existing separately from the "real world," as not *fully* contributing members of society—also plays a part in their trivialization. Further, the content of these designs—often featuring irreverent humor, "low brow" references, children's folklore—relegate them to the category of play rather than the more serious stuff of culture. (And I must admit that I have encountered my fair share of raised eyebrows when I have told people that I am writing a scholarly book about decorated mortarboards.)

Many caps explicitly address the undoubtedly serious *big* issues our world faces today—for example, racial injustice and the ever-worsening climate crisis—but as the previous chapters have made clear, playfulness does not preclude seriousness, and even the silliest of caps are material objects that are intensely "interpersonally and rhetorically dynamic" (Christensen 2017, 269) as they take shape in dialogue with notions of self, education, community, and the unknown future. At the same time, I recognize the irony of articulating my goals in terms of taking these caps *seriously*, especially given the arguments presented in chapter 4 about the discursive role triviality plays in undisciplining the space of commencement and the broader cultural narratives that shape it. Perhaps it is more fruitful to say that, as a folklorist, my key goal for this book has been to engage in the disciplinary tradition of countertrivialization (Fivecoate, Downs, and McGriff 2021).

In their consideration of this disciplinary tradition in folkloristics, Jesse Fivecoate, Kristina Downs, and Meredith McGriff highlight their foundational understanding that "nothing is inherently trivial; rather, triviality is assigned through a *process* of trivialization" (2021, 60, emphasis added). The process of trivialization involves (big or small) acts both of asserting and removing power by drawing and maintaining boundaries around the *significant*. We saw this process at play very clearly, for example, in chapter 3 in the wording of policies, legal decisions, and explanations of school officials and politicians justifying bans on the modification of standard graduation attire.

Approaching triviality as "not an inherent quality but rather an assigned value," Fivecoate, Downs, and McGriff present countertrivialization as a process of working "against the forces in society that create and maintain power differentials between dominant and marginalized groups" (2021, 60). Taking seriously marginalized people and their expressions is part of this process, as is "acknowledging the significance that these forms do hold for the individuals and groups who communicate through them" (2021, 61). Importantly, countertrivialization also involves unpacking the mechanisms by which certain voices are valued and others, consequently, are deemed unimportant, and I have sought to engage in this work of countertrivialization in the pages of this book, drawing not only on the tools of my own discipline (folklore studies), but also other fields of study strongly committed to this work (ethnic studies, queer studies, critical education studies).

This engagement, in turn, necessitates a more thoughtful consideration of the "personal," a concept introduced at the beginning of this book as a key feature of this expressive tradition. The common understanding of these displays as sites of *personal* expression certainly contributes to their trivialization. For example, this designation can work discursively to categorize them as idiosyncratic rather than representative (that is, meaningful to the individual but carrying little significance beyond that).[1] It can also be interpreted as "evidence" of the pathological narcissism of younger generations.[2]

Undoubtedly, the personal is a discursive category embedded in the politics of trivialization. "The personal is political," the feminist rallying cry popularized in the 1960s and 1970s, emerged in direct response to the trivialization of the personal, refusing the naturalized distinctions between the gendered domains of the intimate and the public. Notably, we saw invocations of this idea in many of the social media posts, introduced in chapter 4, marked with the #LatinxGradCaps hashtag, perhaps most explicitly (though certainly not exclusively) in the caption that read "This is political. This is personal. This is all of us" (Latina Rebels 2016a). While destabilizing distinctions between the personal and the political, the private and the public, such a framing makes clear that the personal (like the trivial) is not a stable descriptive category; it is a relational, responsive one. In other words, the personal always takes on meaning in dialogue with *something else*.

At times, as in the case of the feminist slogan and the #LatinxGradCaps hashtag, that *something else* is the political. In these cases, articulations of the personal are already embedded in articulations of the political. The two cannot be extracted from one another. That *something else* can also be the *im*personal, the generic, which, in turn, can be tied to processes of alienation, as addressed in chapter 3. You cannot view decorating one's dorm room door, for example, or putting a bumper sticker on one's car, or embellishing one's mortarboard as acts of personalization unless you understand the broader contexts of these performances to be characterized by *im*personalization. In these contexts of institutionalization or mass production, personalization becomes a strategic mode of claiming space. In these contexts, the power of these acts comes not only through their intentional assertion of distinction from the impersonal but also through their connection to the personhood of the individual. In other words, these acts are meant to communicate something about the individual's view of themselves.

This assertion of self, in turn, should not be understood as existing somehow separately from the context where it finds expression. Putting aspects of the self on display, as addressed in chapter 2, is a process that involves both reflexivity and attention to the broader dynamics of performance. As Jerome Bruner explains, the notion of self "seems to serve as much a *cultural* as an *individual* function" (Bruner 1997, 148, emphasis in original), mediating both interpersonal and institutional encounters. It is no easy task, even at the level of definition, to get a firm grasp on "what it is that, on the one hand, makes selves sufficiently alike to make them intersubjectively communicable, yet sufficiently unique to be distinctively individual" (Bruner 1997, 145). Genres of personal expression, including but certainly not limited to the decorated mortarboards that have been the subject of this book, offer great insight into how these tensions are mediated as these expressions find public audiences.

The taken-for-granted association between the personal and the *individual* self can also be problematized here. Often, the designs of these mortarboards are not only meant to put individual selves on display. As examples introduced throughout chapter 3 and chapter 4 show us, they can also be crafted to intentionally situate the experiences of the individual wearing the cap as part of a larger community experience. When this larger community experience is one characterized by survival and endurance, these material acts of expression can be akin to the narrative genre of testimonios. As Domino Renee Perez explains, "testimonio calls attention to the relationship between the witness and their community. The person providing a testimonio is not speaking for the community; rather, they are speaking about their experiences or what they have witnessed as a member of a specific community. It can be used to assert solidarity" (Perez and Cantú 2022, 152). Norma Cantú further explains how while speaking in the first person, many people who share testimonios "do not see themselves as speaking from an individual perspective and indeed feel they are speaking as a community; it is a communal narrative" (Perez and Cantú 2022, 153). In the expressive acts of sharing testimonios, and I would extend these ideas to many of the caps introduced in this book (consider, as just one example, the cap introduced in chapter 3 that proclaimed "nosotros somos resistencia"), the boundary between the "I" and the "we" is a superficial one. The personal cannot be extracted from the collective, nor should it be.

Even as personalization is intertwined with the process of trivialization, situating one's expression in the domain of the personal simultaneously can work as a powerful rhetorical move, particularly in recent history where we have seen increasing attention to individual narratives in the public culture. This discursive shift away from dominant narratives, Diane Goldstein notes, "has elevated the role of storytellers, witnesses, testimony, life story, and personal experience narrative" (Goldstein 2015, 127). Within this shift, invoking the personal becomes an assertion of authority. And as Amy Shuman (2005) points out, "as an entitled position, personal-experience narratives are relatively uncontested, and knowledge claimed 'from personal experience' is sometimes regarded as more authentic" (Shuman 2005, 153). This widespread view linking entitlement and speaking from personal experience attributes power to the expressive forms that take shape in relation to the personal, particularly "as a corrective to dominant discourses" (Shuman 2005, 11) that naturalize inequities.

This valorization of the personal, however, obscures its constructedness as a discursive category, which in turn fails to recognize the larger-than-personal factors contributing to the meanings this discursive category takes on as personal stories are shared with different audiences. For example, many of the caps in this book feature messages foregrounding the idea of resilience, invoking not only the struggles faced in completing the degree (both within and beyond educational institutions) but also the strength and perseverance needed to overcome these struggles. My conversations with the graduates wearing these caps have revealed a wide array of personal experiences invoked, as well as nuanced motivations for proclaiming this message. Assertions of resilience on customized mortarboards, I have learned through these conversations, are driven by a desire not only to celebrate the ability to persevere amid real challenges but also to recognize the broader social and political forces making resilience necessary in the first place. When an image of a glittery cap proclaiming "resilience" is decontextualized from these experiences and recontextualized into a university's webpage, however, the meaning of the message can be transformed (cf. UNLV Media Relations 2021). Folklorist Dorothy Noyes has traced the rise of "resilience" as what she terms a slogan-concept, "an abstraction that seems to validate concrete realities" (Noyes 2016, 412).[3] When used by those in power, slogan-concepts work, for example, to "distract us from intractable structural problems" (Noyes 2016, 413) and to "discipline behavior" (Noyes 2016, 413). Decontextualized from the specific experiences it references, then re-presented on a university webpage, "resilience" becomes an abstracted moral imperative, one that is visible in domains that extend far beyond higher education. This imperative places the responsibility for "success" onto the individual and away from institutions, and this message is further "authorized" by the cap's association with the personal (even as the situated experiences of the individual are erased).

In studying situated knowledge and the expressive forms communicating that situated knowledge to others, Shuman suggests, it is important not to lose sight of the ongoing, dialogic relationship between the personal and the larger than personal. Applying these ideas to the material expressions of decorated mortarboards, what draws my interest in these caps is not only how they express the personal perspectives of the graduates who wear them. Their significance both includes and extends beyond how they offer a space within the heightened, ritualized context of commencement for graduates to perform the personal, distilling key aspects of themselves in the past, present, and/or future, momentarily, within the blank canvas of the mortarboard. This understanding, in turn, has guided how I have attended to the social contexts of the creation and reception of these caps, for example, and the formal features of the mortarboard designs (e.g., their intertextual engagement with other folk genres and mass or new media content). It has also opened up compelling avenues of inquiry into the ways these caps engage with broader, ongoing conversations about higher education in the United States, conversations grounded in discourses of belonging, citizenship, and the promises of the American dream.

Importantly, taking the dynamic relationship between the personal and the larger than personal as a starting point challenges the false binary of *resistance to* and *affirmation of* institutional values and dominant cultural narratives, and this has been a key touchstone in my thinking about my own engagement in the work of countertrivialization. Such an approach leads us away from the limiting (though nevertheless gratifying) desire to overstate the inherently subversive potential of the personal. As shown in chapter 5, decorated mortarboards do not just push back against the dominant narratives surrounding higher education and its relationship to the American dream. Often, they position individual graduates in alignment with them. Even graduates who understand themselves as being subversive by foregrounding their individual personhood within institutional and cultural spaces they associate with impersonalization, alienation, and exclusion, as introduced in chapter 3 and chapter 4, still often embellish their caps with messages affirming the ideals and hopeful vision embedded within these dominant narratives.

The point here is that there are not distinct categories of caps: ones that perform resistance and ones that do not. Or even distinct categories of graduates: ones that perform resistance and ones that do not. To the contrary, assertions of the personal in the context of mortarboard displays are not de facto subversive, and the boundaries between acts of resistance and acts of affirmation are not clear cut. If these caps reveal anything, it is that individual graduates' relationships with the institutions and broader cultural discourses they must navigate are complicated. As a genre of creative expression tied to the ritual space of commencement, decorated mortarboards are compelling because of the opportunities they open up for individuals to reflect on and communicate their own view of the relationship between the personal and larger-than-personal factors shaping their experiences leading up to the moment of display and their as-of-yet unknown future.

They are also compelling for the points of intersection they help make visible among the diverse graduating students who engage in the practice of customizing their caps, students who bring a wide range of experiences and community memberships to bear on their participation in the ritual of commencement. My intentional approach of including the mortarboard designs and thoughtful insights of graduates with different backgrounds, life experiences, and group affiliations (rather than narrowing the scope of my analysis to a single demographic, for example) highlights how the mortarboard serves as a shared communicative resource within and around the culturally meaningful time of graduation. It also helps us understand how diverse community concerns, values, and histories can intersect through the shared practice of decorating it.[4]

And as the tradition of decorating mortarboards has become more popular, the meanings of these caps are increasingly tied as much to their collectivity as their individuality. Participating in this expressive tradition is much less likely to help one stand out in the crowd now than it would have a few decades ago. At many institutions of higher education, people decorating their caps today realize they are unlikely to be an outlier. Choosing to decorate one's cap is choosing to participate in a shared practice of claiming space. Though individuals seek to perform the personal via their mortarboards, they engage in this optional activity knowingly as part of a collective as well. Like the decorative marginalia in medieval texts described above, the repeated and widespread presence of these decorative embellishments warrant our attention, not as just an amusing novelty but as both individual and collective performances that interact in meaningful ways with the scripted commencement ceremony and the values it represents.

As I write this conclusion in the summer of 2022, there is a great deal of news coverage addressing the worsening decline in college enrollment (cf. Camera 2022; Nietzel 2022; Saul 2022). Attributed in part to the significant disruption brought on by the COVID-19 pandemic in 2020, the causes of this striking decline also include factors that preceded the pandemic, such as lack of public funding for education, which results in rising tuition costs, and increasing skepticism about the value of higher education (Brink 2022; Marken 2019). As university administrators and cultural commentators seek to make sense of this decline and figure out the best way forward, welcoming students' perspectives into the conversation will be an important step. So will being attentive to the ways that students are *already* engaging in this conversation (whether they feel welcomed or not). This book has shown, for example, how graduating students are publicly using the mortarboard, a key symbol of the institution of higher education, to express ambivalence about that institution and the cultural narratives that sustain it. In other words, students "on the ground" are not just thinking about the issues central to the crisis in higher education, they are communicating about them. And as student success in higher education is often measured in terms of crossing the finish line of graduation, these caps offer an entry point into examining students' interpretations of and critical engagement with the narratives of success connected to graduation and the academic accomplishment it represents. Offering insights that both complement and extend beyond the statistical data of enrollment and graduation rates, decorated mortarboards can help us develop more nuanced understandings of how students contextualize their own educational experiences and grapple with the question raised in the introductory chapter: "What good is our education now?" I have sought to lay a foundation for doing this work in this book, though there is much more to explore as this rich expressive tradition continues on and adapts in the future.

Notes

CHAPTER 1: INTRODUCTION

1. I decorated my own cap in coordination with a good friend of mine. We both covered the tops of our mortarboards with wrapping paper and bows. We did not put a great deal of thought into explicitly articulating the meaning of these designs at the time, but looking back, for me it was a gesture to the idea that education is a gift. It also served as a way to mark the close friendship we had shared throughout our college experience. And practically speaking, it made it easier for our families to spot us during the ceremony.

2. I am including the names of interviewees when they have given written consent to have their names included in this manuscript. Being mindful of the potential negative consequences for more vulnerable interviewees (e.g., those who are undocumented) in a fraught political climate, I have chosen to only include first names.

3. The Interdisciplinary Studies program at UNLV allows undergraduate students to pursue two different BA degrees: Social Science Studies and Multidisciplinary Studies. For a Social Science Studies degree, students develop an individualized course of study that integrates coursework from different social science disciplines, including anthropology, gender and sexuality studies, history, political science, psychology, and sociology. For a Multidisciplinary Studies degree, students develop an individualized course of study that integrates coursework from different departments and colleges across the university. According to the program's website, "The degree program in Multidisciplinary Studies is designed for the student who has clear interests and objectives that overlap colleges and/or departments, and whose objectives cannot reasonably be met through existing majors and minors" ("Multidisciplinary Studies" n.d.).

4. The *New York Times* featured one cap that was shaped by these understandings of a college education. This cap included an image of an elephant representing the Republican Party and read, "I Survived College without becoming a DEMOCRAT." The photo of the cap was accompanied by the following words shared by the graduate who wore it: "As one of the only Republicans on my campus (a liberal arts college no less), it was a huge feat that I stayed firm in my beliefs and didn't become a Democrat. That I stood up for my beliefs and stood my ground even with a great deal of backlash is a bigger accomplishment than graduating summa cum laude" (Moore 2019).

5. Interviewed by Brenda Carolina Cruz Gomez in 2017.

6. I did not attend and document at commencement ceremonies in 2020 due to the restrictions of the COVID-19 pandemic.

7. I was not alone in taking a scholarly interest in this rich tradition. Independently in 2017, sociologist Esa Syeed (2018, 2020) similarly began to document and analyze the practice of decorating graduation caps at California State University Long Beach, focusing particularly on the designs and perspectives of students of color.

8. See Harrison et al. (1986) for a quantitative approach to the study of decorated mortarboards and other acts of personal adornment in the context of college commencement ceremonies.

9. Carrie Hertz (2013) offers a beautiful consideration of the many layers of meaning built into the bodily adornment ensembles found in weddings, another rite of passage where dress plays a significant role.

10. An image of this cap is featured in Keaton (2019).

11. The final words of this post reference a quote of unknown origin that has circulated widely in recent years among women's rights and feminist activists. It was also featured on protest signs carried during the 2017 Women's March, another material genre of reflexive and often ludic expression (Saltzman 2020, 46).

12. Carrie Hertz makes a similar point when she writes, "All clothing—whether uniforms or any other genre of dress—operates at a symbolic level within society, allowing individuals to position themselves either in connection with or opposition to any number of perceived social categories" (Hertz 2007, 49).

13. Important human–animal relationships are also marked in the content of many individual mortarboard displays, both through photographs of beloved pets and statements such as "I did it all for my cat" and "I worked hard so my dog can have a better life."

14. In addition to positioning this graduate in relation to his social relationships, it also positions him in terms of time. In my research, I have encountered other examples of decorated caps that link to calendar customs associated with specific annual holidays, including Mother's Day (for spring ceremonies), Christmas (for winter ceremonies), birthdays, and wedding anniversaries. One individual who graduated on St. Patrick's Day included the color green in the design of her cap to mark the holiday and "to tip my hat to my Irish heritage." Another individual whose graduation ceremony took place on May 5, a day popularly associated with drinking, partying, and dressing up as "Mexican" by many non-Latinx students on college campuses, later described his cap in his survey response as including "festive decorations reminiscent of Cinco de Mayo—Confetti, maracas, sombrero."

15. Notably, in all the examples I encountered of this in my research, the person who did decorate the cap was a woman—typically women family members, friends, and girlfriends, though in one situation it was a graduate's supervisor at work.

16. A related but distinct tradition can be found in Germany, where PhD students in the sciences receive a special hat decorated collaboratively by their colleagues in their lab when they complete their degree.

17. Since interviewing Claudia in 2017, I have encountered other caps marking their wearers as part of this specific fandom community, proclaiming other popular phrases from the show including "stay sexy and don't get murdered."

CHAPTER 2: CRAFTING PERFORMANCES OF SELF

1. See Goodson (2018) for a performance-based analysis of the rhetoric of undocumented graduates at undocugrad ceremonies amid shifting political contexts.

2. Patricia Sawin (2004) offers a rich folkloristic examination of the dialogic construction of self.

3. Here, Desiré describes what Uriel Serrano (2020) refers to as an academic homeplace. See also hooks (1990).

4. Desiré's words here resonate with the ideas Norma Marrun presents in her article "Culturally Responsive Teaching across PK-20: Honoring the Historical Naming Practices of Students of Color," in which she argues that "the first step in becoming a multicultural and culturally responsive educator is respecting students' names. When educators mispronounce, Anglicize, or (re)name students of color, they convey a colorblind message to their students that their racial, ethnic, cultural, linguistic, and family and historical backgrounds do not matter in the classroom. This practice frames students of color with non-Eurocentric names as needing to be 'fixed' or 'helping' them 'fit in' through assimilationist practices such as 'Americanizing' their names" (Marrun 2018, 6–7). Making their own name visible on their cap, Desiré referenced their appreciation for the professor who pronounced it correctly while also making visible a refusal to give in to the assimilationist practices structuring many of their educational experiences.

5. See here for the Internet memes Desiré incorporated into their cap's design that spoke to their experiences of struggle:

https://me.me/i/you-i-got-a-bachelors-degree-employers-ok-when-you-9235183

https://me.me/i/when-youre-kinda-slow-but-youre-determined-to-graduate-19662679

https://me.me/i/me-after-finally-graduating-dobby-is-a-free-41-of-c868ab5f4ba04abeab36d0c4c505a147

6. Desiré included these memes into the design of their cap to speak to the celebratory mood that graduation inspired:

https://me.me/i/im-feeling-good-im-feeling-nervous-overwhelmed-everything-butterflies-in-576368a069bf455595f23161ebbcc252

https://www.pinterest.com/pin/427208714636512399/

7. A pseudonym is being used at the interviewee's request.

8. See Wojcik (1995) for further consideration of the punk aesthetic.

9. Martha Sims (2020) addresses similar dynamics of mediating visibility in her study of illness tattoos. See also Candi Cann's consideration of how tattoos serve as "narrative starting points" (Cann 2014, 55), material displays that initiate interpersonal engagement.

CHAPTER 3: DRESS AND THE VISUAL RHETORICS OF BELONGING AND EXCLUSION IN THE COMMENCEMENT RITUAL

1. These experiences are also very well documented in the scholarship of higher education more broadly. See, for example, González (2002), Loo and Rolison (1986), Sedlacek (1987), and Thompson and Fretz (1991).

2. Ray's words here align clearly with Esa Syeed's assertion that "for students of color in particular, who are often misrepresented or marginalized, they may see their caps as one way of making themselves visible" (Syeed 2020, 366).

3. Similar rhetoric was used by another principal who said, "It's always been our tradition that Skyview students graduate in what we call a sea of blue. . . . It's just been Skyview tradition, I guess, is the best way to put it. . . . I think those school traditions are important" (Hoffman 2017).

4. She went on to say: "I'm not going to use crazy colors. I'll be using our school colors. It's respecting myself, family, and elders, and it's also a dedication to those who couldn't get

to this point" (Schorchit 2017). In this case, the integration of school colors was meant to align the graduate with the institution *while* minimizing intertextual gaps (Briggs and Bauman 1992) between the meanings attached to mortarboards as modes of performance within both institutional and community framings.

5. As Bryan McKinley Jones Brayboy reminds us, "Governmental policies and educational policies toward Indigenous peoples are intimately linked around the problematic goal of assimilation" (Brayboy 2005, 429). See also Adams (1995), Lomawaima and McCarty (2002, 2006), and Trafzer, Keller, and Sisquoc (2006).

6. See Brayboy (2004) for a deeper consideration of how American Indian students respond to these stigmatizing contexts by strategically managing their (in)visibility within institutions of higher education.

7. As Rachel Valentina González asserts in her study of the performative dynamics of quinceañera celebrations and social belonging, "Cultural austerity is a social milieu that encourages socialization through common culture that implicitly calls for the scouring of ethnoracial difference from the public sphere for the sake of national unification" (González 2019, 34).

8. I use the phrase "out of place" here to invoke both Kenneth González's research with Chicano students in a primarily white institution (students who commonly voiced feeling "out of place" in these institutional spaces) (González 2002, 203) and Mary Douglas's understanding of the symbolic constructions of dirt as "matter out of place," as something that "offends against order" (Douglas 2003).

9. See also Good (2021).

10. Richard Dyer makes a similar point about the ways in which whiteness becomes synonymous with the universal when he writes: "For those in power in the West, as long as whiteness is felt to be the human condition, then it alone both defines normality and fully inhabits it . . . the equation of being white with being human secures a position of power. White people have power and believe that they think, feel, and act like and for all people; white people, unable to see their particularity, cannot take account of other people's; white people create the dominant images of the world and don't quite see that they thus construct the world in their own image; white people set standards of humanity by which they are bound to succeed and others bound to fail" (Dyer 2005, 12).

11. These dynamics, of course, are not just limited to hair, or even to official dress codes. Louis M. Maraj considers the various ways that "clothing and other (em)bodied rhetorics" are used to "exclude identities—particularly Black identities—from eligibility in campus community" (Maraj 2020, 113).

12. One such cap with a three-dimensional rendering of black hair is on display as part of the History Matters exhibition at the Virginia Museum of History and Culture. This cap was worn in 2018 by Ginai Seabron, the first African American woman to earn a degree in Nanoscience from Virginia Tech ("History Matters" n.d.). The label accompanying this artifact in the physical space of the museum includes this quote from Seabron: "It's not easy at all being the only African American in the room."

13. This sense of not quite fitting undoubtedly informs the increasing demand for and participation in specialty ceremonies (e.g., Black graduations, Latinx graduations, Lavender graduations, undocumented graduations). Because students do not feel affirmed in "traditional" dominant graduation ceremonies, many opt to celebrate on the margins.

14. Mitchell (2018) offers a more in-depth discussion of what she terms "know-your-place aggression."

CHAPTER 4: INTO THE PUBLIC SPHERE: COUNTERING, REARTICULATING, AND REIMAGINING DOMINANT NARRATIVES OF CITIZENSHIP

1. Taking inspiration from this hashtag, I worked in collaboration with Brenda Carolina Cruz Gomez, Claudia Chiang-López, and Nicole Cristina Espinosa to curate a digital exhibit entitled "¡Sí Se Pudo!: The Art and Stories of Latinx Graduation Caps," which highlighted the mortarboard designs and words of Latinx graduates at UNLV (Bock et al. 2019).

2. The term *Latinidad* refers to the geopolitical experience of being Latina/o/x that transcends national and geographic borders. Beyond the shared nature of this experience, the term "also contains within it the complexities and contradictions of immigration, (post) (neo)colonialism, race, color, legal status, class, nation, language, and the politics of location" (Rodríguez 2003, 9–10).

3. Although this text is no longer posted on the Latina Rebels Facebook page, it can still be found in the Remezcla article "9 Young Central American Creatives and Thought Leaders You Should Be Following" (Simón 2016).

4. Originating in the online queer Latinx community, use of the term *Latinx* has become more widespread, though it remains contentious. As Catalina (Kathleen) M. De Onís notes in "What's in an 'X'? An Exchange about the Politics of 'Latinx,'" "Some individuals and communities readily adopt and advocate for increased usage of 'Latinx,' arguing for its transgressive sexual, gender, and language politics. Meanwhile, others express hesitancy or reject usages of 'x' altogether, maintaining that the signifier symbolizes linguistic imperialism, poses pronunciation problems, and alienates non-English-speaking im/migrants" (De Onís 2017, 79).

5. The term *chingona* is often used to refer to a "badass woman" (Aguirre 2017). Mexican American writer Sandra Cisneros has played a significant role is rearticulating the meaning of the term, which loosely translates to "fucker" in English. The masculine version of the term describes someone who dominates through sexual penetration. According to Cisneros, "I had to take that word back [because] I felt that that word was a word that's used against women and gays. . . . I wanted to find a positive way to say 'a woman who is on her path and who is powerful and is not being defined by a man but is being defined as a woman on her own path, on her own direction, on her own intuitive powers'" (quoted in Moreno 2017). See also Gloria Anzaldúa (2007) and Octavio Paz's (1961) writings on "la Chingada." As sociologist Julie Bettie explains, the term *chola/o* "describes a Mexican-American street style that sometimes marks identification with gangs, but it also can mark merely racial/ethnic belonging" (Bettie 2000, 9). It has historically carried negative associations with criminality and being lower class. See also Castro (2001).

6. I draw here on Rachel Valentina González's work on what she terms "quinceañera style," which considers these dynamics particularly in relation to American quinceañera practice (González 2019).

7. See also Delgado-Gaitan (1994), Heath (1983), Kiyama and Rios-Aguilar (2017), Matos (2015), Muñoz and Maldonado (2012), Solorzano and Yosso (2002), Yosso (2005), and Zalaquett (2006).

8. Pineda and Sowards (2007) offer a more in-depth examination of the visual rhetorics of flag waving within contexts of immigration protests and rallies in the United States. See also Martínez's analysis of the symbolic role flags play in collective performances of Puerto Rican culture (2017).

9. This phrase is used often in Costa Rica and carries many meanings, including "hello," "good-bye," "thank you," and "it's all good," among others (Maney 2016).

10. See Chumakov (2016).

11. "¡Sí se puede!" was the rallying cry of the United Farmworkers Union in the 1970s, and since that time it has been adopted by many groups and movements fighting for Latina/o/x rights in the United States. The English equivalent, "yes we can," served as the slogan for presidential candidate Barack Obama's campaign in 2008.

12. Penial E. Joseph (2016) offers an overview of the powerful historical resonance of the raised fist in the United States.

13. Literally translated as "trout," *trucha* is also slang for "be careful" or "watch out."

14. González-Martín draws upon the work of Norma Cantú (2001) in blurring this distinction.

15. Lynne McNeill (2020) offers further consideration of the folkloric characteristics of the hashtag.

CHAPTER 5: UNDISCIPLINING GRADUATION

1. In 2015, the verb form of *adult* was nominated by the American Dialect Society for the year's most creative new term.

2. My own thinking on how decorated mortarboards call attention has been greatly informed by Dorothy Noyes's (2016) consideration of the aesthetic dimensions of organizing attention in vernacular expression.

3. See also the special issue of the *Journal of Folklore Research* on "Creating from the Margins: Precarity and the Study of Folklore," edited by Sarah M. Gordon and Benjamin Gatling (2021).

CHAPTER 6: CONCLUSION

1. Indeed, Fivecoate, Downs, and McGriff present invocations of the category of the personal as an example of trivialization, referencing specifically "when someone employs the phrase 'that's just anecdotal' in response to another person using personal experience as evidence in an argument." They assert: "The phrase 'just anecdotal' is a rhetorical device that trivializes lived experience; it is meant to undermine the authority one has in properly claiming knowledge of how the world works and to trivialize how individuals and groups place themselves in that world and make sense of it" (Fivecoate, Downs, and McGriff 2021, 60).

2. I encountered this idea during casual conversations with different people about the general topic of my research. In these conversations, my interlocutors drew connections between people decorating their mortarboards and their view of the problematic nature of "selfie culture" on social media.

3. See also Horigan (2018).

4. I owe thanks to the anonymous reviewer who helped me articulate these ideas more clearly.

References

Adams, David Wallace. 1995. *Education for Extinction: American Indians and the Boarding School Experience, 1875–1928*. Lawrence: University Press of Kansas.

Adams, James Truslow. 1931. *The Epic of America*. Boston: Little, Brown.

Aguas, Evangeline. 2021. "Queer Interruptions: Delay, Belatedness and Wasted Time." https://vimeo.com/showcase/8628856/video/566886467.

Aguirre, Angela. 2017. "How I Define My Chingona Fire." *Huffington Post*. Updated January 25, 2017. https://www.huffingtonpost.com/entry/how-i-define-my-chingona-fire_us_5887de69e4b0a53ed60c6a35.

Ahmed, Sara. 2012. *On Being Included*. Durham: Duke University Press.

Anzaldúa, Gloria. 2007. *Borderlands/La Frontera: The New Mestiza*, 3rd ed. San Francisco: Aunt Lute.

Bakhtin, Mikhail. 1984. *Rabelais and His World*. Bloomington: Indiana University Press.

Bakhtin, Mikhail M., and Michael Holquist. 1981. *The Dialogic Imagination: Four Essays*. Austin: University of Texas Press.

Bakhtin, Mikhail M., Michael Holquist, Vern McGee, and Caryl Emerson. 1986. "The Problem with Speech Genres." In *Speech Genres and Other Late Essays*. Austin: University of Texas Press.

Bamberg, Michael, and Alexandra Georgakopoulou. 2008. "Small Stories as a New Perspective in Narrative and Identity Analysis." *Text and Talk* 28 (3): 377–396.

Bauman, Richard. 1977. *Verbal Art as Performance*. Rowley, MA: Newbury House Publishers.

Bauman, Richard, and Charles L. Briggs. 1990. "Poetics and Performances as Critical Perspectives on Language and Social Life." *Annual Review of Anthropology* 19 (1): 59–88.

Beresin, Anna. 2015. "Pen Tapping: Forbidden Folklore." *Journal of Folklore and Education* 2: 19–21. https://jfepublications.org/article/pen-tapping/.

Berlinger, Gabrielle Anna. 2017. *Framing Sukkot: Tradition and Transformation in Jewish Vernacular Architecture*. Bloomington: Indiana University Press.

Bettie, Julie. 2000. "Women without Class: Cholas, Trash, and the Presence/Absence of Class Identity." *Signs* 26 (1): 1–35.

Bock, Sheila. 2017. "Ku Klux Kasserole and Strange Fruit Pies: A Shouting Match at the Border in Cyberspace." *Journal of American Folklore* 130 (516): 142–165.

Bock, Sheila, Brenda Carolina Cruz Gomez, Claudia Chiang-López, and Nicole Cristina Espinosa. 2019. "¡Sí Se Pudo!: The Art and Stories of Latinx Graduation Caps." Digital exhibit on display at the Lied Library, University of Nevada, Las Vegas. https://digitalscholarship.unlv.edu/lib_latinx_grad_caps/.

Boven, David T. 2009. "American Universities' Departure from the Academic Costume Code." *Transactions of the Burgon Society* 9: 156–174.

Brayboy, Bryan McKinley Jones. 2004. "Hiding in the Ivy: American Indian Students and Visibility in Elite Educational Settings." *Harvard Educational Review* 74 (2): 125–152.

Brayboy, Bryan McKinley Jones. 2005. "Toward a Tribal Critical Race Theory in Education." *Urban Review* 37 (5): 425–446.

Briggs, Charles L., and Richard Bauman. 1992. "Genre, Intertextuality, and Social Power." *Journal of Linguistic Anthropology* 2 (2): 131–172.

https://doi.org/10.7330/9781646425259.c007

Brink, Meghan. 2022. "Public Opinion on Value of Higher Ed Remains Mixed." *Inside Higher Ed.* July 12, 2022. https://www.insidehighered.com/news/2022/07/12/most-americans-skeptical-value-college-degree.

Bronner, Simon J. 2012. *Campus Traditions: Folklore from the Old-time College to the Modern Mega-University.* Jackson: University Press of Mississippi.

Bruner, Jerome. 1997. "A Narrative Model of Self-Construction." *Annals of the New York Academy of Sciences* 818 (1): 145–161.

Buccitelli, Anthony Bak. 2012. "Performance 2.0: Observations toward a Theory of the Digital Performance of Folklore." In *Folk Culture in the Digital Age: The Emergent Dynamics of Human Interaction*, edited by Trevor J. Blank, 60–84. Logan: Utah State University Press.

Calvan, Bobby Caina. 2017. "Bill Would Allow Native Graduates to Wear Regalia." *The Spokesman-Review*, February 24, 2017. http://www.spokesman.com/stories/2017/feb/24/bill-would-allow-native-graduates-to-wear-regalia/.

Camera, Lauren. 2022. "College Enrollment Declines Are Here to Stay." *US News*, May 26, 2022. https://www.usnews.com/news/education-news/articles/2022-05-26/college-enrollment-declines-are-here-to-stay.

Camille, Michael. 1992. *Image on the Edge: The Margins of Medieval Art.* London: Reaktion Books.

Cann, Candi K. 2014. *Virtual Afterlives: Grieving the Dead in the Twenty-First Century.* Lexington: University Press of Kentucky.

Cantú, Norma Elia. 2001. "Whose Story Is It Anyway?: Autobiography on the Border." In NACCS Annual Conference Proceedings, 129–145. https://scholarworks.sjsu.edu/cgi/viewcontent.cgi?article=1039&context=naccs.

Castro, Rafaela G. 2001. "Cholos (-as)." In *Chicano Folklore: A Guide to the Folktales, Traditions, Rituals, and Religious Practices of Mexican Americans*, edited by Rafaela G. Castrom, 54–55. Oxford: Oxford University Press.

Chang, Aurora. 2011. "Undocumented to Hyperdocumented: A Jornada of Protection, Papers, and PhD Status." *Harvard Educational Review* 81 (3): 508–521.

Chavez, Leo R. 2013. *The Latino Threat: Constructing Immigrants, Citizens, and the Nation*, 2nd ed. Stanford: Stanford University Press.

Christensen, Danille Elise. 2011. "'Look at Us Now!': Scrapbooking, Regimes of Value, and the Risks of (Auto)ethnography." *Journal of American Folklore* 124 (493): 175–210.

Christensen, Danille Elise. 2016. "(Not) Going Public: Mediating Reception and Managing Visibility in Contemporary Scrapbook Performance." In *Material Vernaculars: Objects, Images, and Their Social Worlds*, edited by Jason Baird Jackson, 40–104. Bloomington: Indiana University Press.

Christensen, Danille Elise. 2017. "Materializing the Everyday: 'Safe' Scrapbooks, Aesthetic Mess, and the Rhetorics of Workmanship." *Journal of Folklore Research* 54 (3): 233–284.

Chumakov. 2016. "Con el nopal en la Frente." *USC Digital Folklore Archives.* May 12, 2016. http://folklore.usc.edu/?p=33460.

Colón, Laura (@laura_colon). 2017. Instagram post. May 20. https://www.instagram.com/p/BUVtNYcDIff/.

Cullen, Jim. 2003. *The American Dream: A Short History of the Idea That Shaped a Nation.* Oxford: Oxford University Press.

de Certeau, Michel. 1984. *The Practice of Everyday Life.* Translated by Steven Rendall. Berkeley: University of California Press.

De Onís, Catalina (Kathleen) M. 2017. "What's in an 'X'? An Exchange about the Politics of 'Latinx.'" *Chiricù Journal: Latina/o Literature, Art, and Culture* 1 (2): 78–91.

Delgado Bernal, D. 2001. "Living and Learning Pedagogies of the Home: The Mestiza Consciousness of Chicana Students." *International Journal of Qualitative Studies in Education* 14 (5): 623–639.

Delgado-Gaitan, C. 1994. "Consejos: The Power of Cultural Narratives." *Anthropology and Education Quarterly* 25 (3): 298–316.

Deppermann, Arnulf. 2015. "Positioning." In *The Handbook of Narrative Analysis*, edited by Anna de Fina and Alexandra Georgiakopoulou, 369–387. West Sussex: John Wiley & Sons.

Dick, Hilary Parsons. 2011. "Language and Migration in the United States." *Annual Review of Anthropology* 40: 227–240.

Douglas, Mary. 2003. *Purity and Danger: An Analysis of Concepts of Pollution and Taboo.* London: Routledge.

"Dow Protest at Graduation." 1967. University of Wisconsin-Madison Archives Collections. https://digital.library.wisc.edu/1711.dl/UWGBYXGNPIL5N8L.

Dundes, Alan. 1966. "Metafolklore and Oral Literary Criticism." *The Monist* 50: 505–516.

Dundes, Alan. 1969. "Thinking Ahead: A Folkloristic Reflection of the Future Orientation in American Worldview." *Anthropological Quarterly* 42 (2): 53–72.

Dundes, Alan. 1971. "Folk Ideas as Units of Worldview." *Journal of American Folklore* 84 (331): 93–103.

Dundes, Alan. 2004. "'As the Crow Flies': A Straightforward Study of Lineal Worldview in American Folk Speech." In *What Goes Around Comes Around: The Circulation of Proverbs in Contemporary Life*, edited by Kimberly J. Lou, Peter Tokofsky, and Stephen D. Winick, 171–187. Logan: Utah State University Press.

Dundes, Alan, and Carl R. Pagter. (1978) 1992. *Work Hard and You Shall Be Rewarded: Urban Folklore from the Paperwork Empire*. Detroit: Wayne State University Press.

Dundes, Alan, and Carl R. Pagter. 1987. *When You're Up to Your Ass in Alligators: More Urban Folklore from the Paperwork Empire*. Detroit: Wayne State University Press.

Dundes Renteln, Alison. 2004. *The Cultural Defense.* Oxford: Oxford University Press.

Dyer, Richard. 2005. "The Matter of Whiteness." In *White Privilege: Essential Readings on the Other Side of Racism*, 2nd ed., edited by Paula Rothenberg, 9–13. New York: Worth Publishers.

Eldridge, Samantha (@DCSamantha). 2019. Twitter post. June 3. https://twitter.com/dc samantha/status/1135634029007462400?s=46&t=H9eOCByj_-vbGHHdxVIR2A.

Fivecoate, Jesse A., Kristina Downs, and Meredith A. E. McGriff. 2021. "The Politics of Trivialization." In *Advancing Folkloristics*, edited by Jesse A. Fivecoate, Kristina Downs, and Meredith A. E. McGriff, 59–76. Bloomington: Indiana University Press.

Flores, William Vincent, and Rina Benmayor, eds. 1997. *Latino Cultural Citizenship: Claiming Identity, Space, and Rights.* Boston: Beacon.

Fort, Kate. 2014. "Letter from NARF, ACLU, and California Indian Legal Services Regarding Wearing Eagle Feather at Graduation." Turtle Talk. June 17, 2014. https://turtletalk.wordpress.com/2014/06/17/letter-from-narf-aclu-and-california -indian-legal-services-regarding-wearing-eagle-feathers-at-graduation/.

Fort, Kate. 2015. "Magistrate Decision in Griffith v. Caney Valley Public Schools." Turtle Talk. May 20, 2015. https://turtletalk.blog/2015/05/20/magistrate-decision-in -griffith-v-caney-valley-public-schools/.

Foucault, Michel. 1975. *Discipline and Punish: The Birth of the Prison.* Translated by A. Sheridan. New York: Vintage Books.

Fujii, Jocelyn. 1999. "The Many Messages of the Lei." *New York Times.* March 28, 1999. https://www.nytimes.com/1999/03/28/travel/the-many-messages-of-the-lei.html.

Gabbert, Lisa, and Anton Salud. 2009. "On Slanderous Words and Bodies Out-of-Control: Hospital Humor and the Medical Carnivalesque." In *The Body in Medical Culture*, edited by Elizabeth Klaver, 209–227. Albany: State University of New York Press.

Goldstein, Diane. 2015. "Vernacular Turns: Narrative, Local Knowledge, and the Changed Context of Folklore." *Journal of American Folklore* 128 (508): 125–145.

González, Kenneth P. 2002. "Campus Culture and the Experiences of Chicano Students in a Predominantly White University." *Urban Education* 37 (2): 193–218.

González, Rachel Valentina. 2019. *Quinceañera Style: Social Belonging and Latinx Consumer Identities*. Austin: University of Texas Press.

González-Martín, Rachel. 2019. "Crossing the Stage." Conference paper presented at the American Folklore Society Annual Meeting, Baltimore, MD.

González-Martín, Rachel. 2020. "Latinx Publics: Self-Documentation and Latina Youth Activists." *Journal of American Folklore* 133 (530): 430–451.

Good, Crystal. 2021. "Meet the 5 Women Uprooting White Beauty Standards and White Supremacy in West Virginia." *Scalawag*. May 11, 2021. https://scalawagmagazine.org/2021/05/wv-crown-act-hair-law/.

Goodson, Christopher. 2018. "The Undocu-Graduation (2015–17): The Performance of Citizenship and Anti-Ritual." *Theatre Topics* 28 (2): 151–158.

Gordon, Sarah M., and Benjamin Gatling, eds. 2021. "Special Issue: Creating from the Margins: Precarity and the Study of Folklore." *Journal of Folklore Research* 58 (3).

Gose, Ben. 1995. "Wearing Kente Stoles at Commencement." *The Chronicle of Higher Education*. May 6, 1995. https://www.chronicle.com/article/wearing-kente-stoles-at-commencement/.

Grundlingh, Lezandra. 2018. "Memes as Speech Acts." *Social Semiotics* 28 (2): 147–168.

Gutierrez, Lisa. 2016. "Native American High-Schoolers Who Want to Wear Eagle Feathers for Graduation Take Their Cause to Court." *Kansas City Star*. May 6, 2016. https://www.kansascity.com/news/nation-world/national/article76052302.html.

Halberstam, J. Jack. 2005. *In A Queer Time and Place: Transgender Bodies, Subcultural Lives*. New York: New York University Press.

Halberstam, J. Jack. 2011. *The Queer Art of Failure*. Durham, NC: Duke University Press.

Hanson, Sandra L., and John Kenneth White. 2016. "Introduction." In *The Latino/a American Dream*, edited by Sandra L. Hanson and John Kenneth White, 1–17. College Station: Texas A&M University Press.

Hargreaves-Mawdsley, William Norman. 1978. *A History of Academical Dress in Europe*. Westport, CT: Greenwood Press.

Harrison, Albert A., Robert Sommer, Margaret H. Rucker, and Michael Moore. 1986. "Standing Out From the Crowd: Personalization of Graduation Attire." *Adolescence* 21 (84): 863–874.

Haynes, Deborah J. 2008. "Bakhtin and the Visual Arts." In *A Companion to Art Theory*, edited by Paul Smith and Carolyn Wilde, 292–302. Oxford: Blackwell Publishing.

Heath, Shirley Brice. 1983. *Ways with Words: Language, Life and Work in Communities and Classrooms*. Cambridge: Cambridge University Press.

Henn, Danielle. 2018. "A Pedagogy of Making Do." *Journal of Folklore and Education* 5 (2):161–169. https://jfepublications.org/article/a-pedagogy-of-making-do/.

Hertz, Carrie. 2007. "The Uniform: As Material, as Symbol, as Negotiated Object." *Midwestern Folklore* 32 (1/2): 43–56.

Hertz, Carrie. 2013. "White Wedding Dress in the Midwest." PhD diss., Indiana University.

"History Matters." n.d. Virginia Museum of History and Culture. https://virginiahistory.org/exhibitions/history-matters. Accessed August 8, 2022.

Hoffman, Mark. 2017. "Billings Students Back Bill That Would Allow Native American Dress at High School Graduations." *Billings Gazette*. March 1, 2017. https://

billingsgazette.com/news/local/education/billings-students-back-bill-that-would
-allow-native-american-dress/article_5f4f615e-66a7-5508-8caa-6c43189b03d9.html.

hooks, bell. 1990. *Yearning: Race, Gender, and Cultural Politics*. Boston, MA: South End Press.

Horigan, Kate Parker. 2018. *Consuming Katrina: Public Disaster and Personal Narrative*. Jackson: University Press of Mississippi.

Hurtado, Sylvia. 1992. "The Campus Racial Climate: Contexts of Conflict." *Journal of Higher Education* 63 (5): 539–569.

Hurtado, Sylvia, and Luis Ponjuan. 2005. "Latino Educational Outcomes and the Campus Climate." *Journal of Hispanic Higher Education* 4 (3): 235–251.

"I Have 3 Dollars." n.d. Know Your Meme. https://knowyourmeme.com/memes/i-have
-3-dollars. Accessed November 17, 2021.

Ivey, Bill. 2018. *Rebuilding an Enlightened World: Folklorizing America*. Bloomington: Indiana University Press.

Joseph, Penial E. 2016. "The Many Meanings of a Fist." *Chronicle Review*. May 18, 2016. https://www.chronicle.com/article/The-Many-Meanings-of-a-Fist/236509.

Kapchan, Deborah. 2003. "Performance." In *Eight Words for the Study of Expressive Culture*, edited by Burt Feintuch. Urbana: University of Illinois Press.

Keaton, Kevin. 2019. "Ari Kravitz: Transitioning in College." *1870 Magazine*. May 31, 2019. https://1870mag.com/ari-kravitz-transitioning-in-college/.

Kelley, Greg. 2020. *Unruly Audience: Folk Interventions in Popular Media*. Logan: Utah State University Press.

Kirshenblatt-Gimblett, Barbara. 1998. *Destination Culture: Tourism, Museums, and Heritage*. Berkeley: University of California Press.

Kiyama, Judy Marquez, and Cecilia Rios-Aguilar, eds. 2017. *Funds of Knowledge in Higher Education: Honoring Students' Cultural Experiences and Resources as Strengths*. New York: Routledge.

Lankshear, Colin, and Michele Knobel. 2002. "Steps toward a Pedagogy of Tactics." Keynote paper prepared for the National Council of English Teachers' Assembly for Research Mid-Winter Conference, New York. http://everydayliteracies.net/files
/pedtact.html.

Latina Rebels (@latinarebels). 2016a. Instagram post. May 13. https://www.instagram
.com/p/BFW_p8OLq1p/.

Latina Rebels (@latinarebels). 2016b. Instagram post. May 14. https://www.instagram
.com/p/BFZfA49Lq_1/.

Latina Rebels (@latinarebels). 2016c. Instagram post. May 15. https://www.instagram
.com/p/BFcYVoVLqy4/.

Latina Rebels (@latinarebels). 2016d. Instagram post. May 19. https://www.instagram
.com/p/BFnCCksLq0Y/.

Latina Rebels (@latinarebels). 2016e. Instagram post. June 13. https://www.instagram
.com/p/BGmGn9qLq7q/.

Latina Rebels (@latinarebels). 2017. Instagram post. March 12. https://www.instagram
.com/p/BRjBLC_g3ax/.

Lee, Dorothy. (1959) 1968. "Codifications of Reality: Lineal and Nonlineal." In *Every Man His Way: Readings in Cultural Anthropology*, edited by Alan Dundes, 329–343. Englewood Cliffs, NJ: Prentice-Hall. Originally published in *Freedom and Culture*.

Leonard, Gardner Cotrell. 2010. *The Cap and Gown in America: Reprinted from the University Magazine for December, 1893 (1896)*. Albany, NY: Cotrell Leonard.

Lomawaima, K. Tsianina, and Teresa L. McCarty. 2002. "When Tribal Sovereignty Challenges Democracy: American Indian Education and the Democratic Ideal." *American Educational Research Journal* 39 (2): 279–305.

Lomawaima, K. Tsianina, and Teresa L. McCarty. 2006. *"To Remain an Indian": Lessons in Democracy from a Century of Native American Education.* New York: Teachers College Press.

Longhi, Lorraine. 2019. "ACLU Defends Native American Student's Right to Wear Beaded Cap to Graduation." *Arizona Republic.* May 15, 2019. https://www.azcentral.com/story/news/local/surprise-education/2019/05/15/aclu-defends-sioux-students-right-wear-beaded-cap-graduation/3683173002/.

Loo, Chalsa M., and Garry Rolison. 1986. "Alienation of Ethnic Minority Students at a Predominantly White University." *Journal of Higher Education* 57 (1): 58–77.

Magolda, Peter Mark. 2003. "Saying Good-bye: An Anthropological Examination of a Commencement Ritual." *Journal of College Student Development* 44 (6): 779–796.

Maney, Andrew. 2016. "Pura Vida." USC Digital Folklore Archives. May 12, 2016. http://folklore.usc.edu/?p=34094.

Manning, Kathleen. 2000. *Rituals, Ceremonies, and Cultural Meaning in Higher Education.* Westport, CT: Greenwood Publishing Group.

Maraj, Louis M. 2020. *Black or Right: Anti/Racist Campus Rhetorics.* Louisville: University Press of Colorado.

Marken, Stephanie. 2019. "Half in U.S. Now Consider College Education Very Important." *Gallup.* https://www.gallup.com/education/272228/half-consider-college-education-important.aspx.

Marrun, Norma. 2018. "Culturally Responsive Teaching across PK-20: Honoring the Historical Naming Practices of Students of Color." *Taboo: The Journal of Culture and Education* 17 (3): 6–25.

Marrun, Norma Angelica. 2020. "'My Mom Seems to Have a *Dicho* for Everything!': Family Engagement in the College Success of Latina/o Students." *Journal of Latinos and Education* 19 (2): 164–180.

Martínez, Daniel E., Jeremy Slack, Alex E. Chávez, and Scott Whiteford. 2016. "'The American Dream': Walking toward and Deporting It." In *The Latino/a American Dream*, edited by Sandra L. Hanson and John Kenneth White, 88–98. College Station: Texas A&M University Press.

Martínez, Elena. 2017. "¡Que Bonita Bandera! Place, Space, and Identity as Expressed with the Puerto Rican Flag." In *Public Performances: Studies in the Carnivalesque and Ritualesque*, edited by Jack Santino, 113–132. Logan: Utah State University Press.

Matos, J. M. D. 2015. "La Familia: The Important Ingredient for Latina/o College Student Engagement and Persistence." *Equity and Excellence* 48 (3): 436–453.

McNeill, Lynne S. 2020. "Classifying #BlackLivesMatter: Genre and Form in Digital Folklore." In *Folklore and Social Media*, edited by Andrew Peck and Trevor J. Blank, 179–187. Logan: Utah State University Press.

Mitchell, Koritha. 2018. "Identifying White Mediocrity and Know-Your-Place Aggression: A Form of Self-Care." *African American Review* 51 (4): 253–262.

Monette, Melvin. 2015. "Letter to Larry P. Nybladh." Turtle Talk. January 14, 2015. https://turtletalk.files.wordpress.com/2015/02/eagle-feather-packet.pdf.

Moore, Lela. 2019. "Wearing Their Hearts on Their Graduation Caps." *New York Times.* June 11, 2019. https://www.nytimes.com/2019/06/11/reader-center/graduation-caps-messages.html.

Moreno, Carolina. 2017. "Sandra Cisneros Defines What It Means to Be a Chingona." *Huffington Post.* September 6, 2017. https://www.huffingtonpost.com/entry/sandra-cisneros-chingona-definition_us_59ae10ade4b0dfaafcf2030b.

"Multidisciplinary Studies." n.d. University of Nevada, Las Vegas Interdisciplinary, Gender, and Ethnic Studies. https://www.unlv.edu/interdisciplinary/multidisciplinary-studies. Accessed June 1, 2022.

Muñoz, Susana María, and Marta María Maldonado. 2012. "Counterstories of College Persistence by Undocumented Mexicana Students: Navigating Race, Class, Gender, and Legal Status." *International Journal of Qualitative Studies in Education* 25 (3): 293–315.

Nathan, Rebekah. 2006. *My Freshman Year: What a Professor Learned by Becoming a Student.* New York: Penguin Books.

Native Lives Matter (@ NLMCoalition). 2015. Twitter post. January 21. https:// twitter.com/nlmcoalition/status/558126305582260225?s=46&t=H9eOCByj_ -vbGHHdxVIR2A.

Negrón-Gonzales, Genevieve. 2014. "Undocumented, Unafraid & Unapologetic: Re-articulatory Practices & Migrant Youth 'Illegality.'" *Latino Studies* 12 (2): 259–228.

Nietzel, Michael T. 2022. "News Report: The College Enrollment Decline Worsened This Spring." *Forbes.* May 26, 2022. https://www.forbes.com/sites/michaeltnietzel/2022 /05/26/new-report-the-college-enrollment-decline-has-worsened-this-spring/?sh= 5a9a5f2124e0.

"Non-Traditional Students." n.d. University of Nevada, Las Vegas. https://www.unlv.edu /nontraditional. Accessed November 17, 2021.

Noyes, Dorothy. 2016. "Aesthetic Is the Opposite of Anaesthetic: On Tradition and Attention." In *Humble Theory: Folklore's Grasp on Social Life*, 127–178. Bloomington: Indiana University Press.

Ouellet, Nicky. 2017. "Native Regalia Laws Tested, Brings Change in Kalispell." Montana Public Radio Here and Now. June 5, 2017. https://www.mtpr.org/post/native -regalia-law-tested-brings-change-kalispell.

Oversen, Kylie. 2014. "Letter to Principals Kasowski and Arason." Turtle Talk. January 7, 2014. https://turtletalk.files.wordpress.com/2015/02/eagle-feather-packet.pdf.

Oxford Reference. n.d. "Discipline." Accessed May 3, 2023. https://www.oxfordreference .com/display/10.1093/oi/authority.20110803095721587;jsessionid= A60922C9F8651EC96114BDFF9A7366EF.

Parédez, Deborah. 2009. *Selenidad: Selena, Latinos, and the Performance of Memory.* Durham, NC: Duke University Press.

Paz, Octavio. 1961. *The Labyrinth of Solitude.* Translated by Lysander Kemp. New York: Grove.

Perez, Domino Renee, and Norma E. Cantú. 2022. "Talking Testimonio: Telling History and Memory." *Journal of American Folklore* 135 (536): 150–163.

Perry, Andre. 2019. "Stay Out of My Hair!" *The Hechinger Report.* March 5, 2019. https:// hechingerreport.org/stay-out-of-my-hair/.

Peterson, Mark Allen. 2005. "Performing Media: Toward an Ethnography of Intertextuality." In *Media Anthropology*, edited by Eric W. Rothenbuhler and Mihai Coman, 129–138. Thousand Oaks, CA: Sage Publications.

Pewewardy, Cornel, and Bruce Frey. 2002. "Surveying the Landscape: Perceptions of Multicultural Support Services and Racial Climate at a Predominantly White University." *Journal of Negro Education* 71 (1): 77–95.

Pineda, Richard D., and Stacey K. Sowards. 2007. "Flag Waving as Visual Argument: 2006 Immigration Demonstrations and Cultural Citizenship." *Argumentation and Advocacy* 43:164–174.

Platt, R. Eric, and Lauren Huffman Walker. 2019. "Regalia Remembered: Exploring the History and Symbolic Significance of Higher Education Academic Costume." *American Educational History Journal* 46 (1): 125–141.

Puwar, Nirmal. 2004. *Space Invaders: Race, Gender and Bodies Out of Place.* Oxford: Berg.

Raheja, Michelle H. 2011. *Reservation Reelism: Redfacing, Visual Sovereignty, and Representations of Native Americans in Film.* Lincoln: University of Nebraska Press.

Reid, Landon D., and Phanikiran Radhakrishnan. 2003. "Race Matters: The Relation between Race and General Campus Climate." *Cultural Diversity and Ethnic Minority Psychology* 9 (3): 263–275.

Remezcla Estaff. 2017. "The #ImmiGrad Hashtag Is a Testament to the Sacrifices Parents Make for Their Children." Remezcla. May 22, 2017. http://remezcla.com/lists /culture/immigrad-parents-sacrifice/.

Reuters. 2015. "Native American Student Sues School District over Right to Wear Feather at Graduation." *HuffPost.* June 2, 2015. https://www.huffpost.com/entry/christian -titman-lawsuit_n_7490464.

Rodríguez, Juana María. 2003. *Queer Latinidad: Identity Practices, Discursive Spaces.* New York: NYU Press.

Rosencranz, Mary Lou. 1972. *Clothing Concepts: A Social-Psychological Approach.* New York: Macmillan.

Saltzman, Rachelle Hope, ed. 2020. *Pussy Hats, Politics, and Public Protest.* Jackson: University Press of Mississippi.

San Emeterio, Neus Ribas. 2016. "The Role of Clothing in Rites of Passage." *Datatèxtil* 34: 60–69.

Santino, Jack. 1986. "The Folk Assemblage of Autumn: Tradition and Creativity in Halloween Folk Art." In *Folk Art and Art Worlds,* edited by John Michael Vlach and Simon Bronner, 151–169. Ann Arbor, MI: UMI Research Press.

Saul, Stephanie. 2022. "College Enrollment Drops, Even as the Pandemic's Effects Ebb." *New York Times.* May 26, 2022. https://www.nytimes.com/2022/05/26/us/college -enrollment.html.

Sawin, Patricia. 2004. *Listening for a Life: A Dialogic Ethnography of Bessie Eldreth Through Her Songs and Stories.* Logan: Utah State University Press.

Schaefer, Jason. 2015. "Letter to Grand Forks Public School Administration." Turtle Talk. January 13, 2015. https://turtletalk.files.wordpress.com/2015/02/eagle-feather -packet.pdf.

Schmitt, Casey R. 2013. "Asserting Tradition: Rhetoric of Tradition and the Defense of Chief Illiniwek." In *Tradition in the Twenty-First Century: Locating the Role of the Past in the Present,* edited by Trevor J. Blank and Robert Glenn Howard, 100–122. Logan: Utah State University Press.

Schorchit, Nicolle. 2017. "Students Demand Right to Wear Native Regalia at Graduation." *NEA News.* June 29, 2017. https://www.nea.org/advocating-for-change/new-from -nea/students-demand-right-wear-native-regalia-graduation.

Sedlacek, William E. 1987. "Black Students on White Campuses: 20 Years of Research." *Journal of College Student Personnel* 28: 484–495.

Seelye, Katharine Q. 2018. "Roaring Protests of Commencements Past Make Way for a More Subdued Stand." *New York Times.* May 31, 2018. https://www.nytimes.com /2018/05/31/us/commencement-college-protests.html.

Seif, H. 2011. "'Unapologetic and Unafraid': Immigrant Youth Come Out from the Shadows." *New Directions for Child and Adolescent Development* 134: 59–75.

Seif, H., C. Ullman, and G. Núñez-Mchiri. 2014. "Mexican (Im)migrant Students and Education: Constructions of and Resistance to 'Illegality.'" *Latino Studies* 12 (2): 172–193.

Serebriany, Zoey. 2019. "Right to Regalia: Let Those Feathers Fly at Graduation." *Lakota People's Law Project.* June 3, 2019. https://www.lakotalaw.org/news/2019-06-03/right -to-regalia.

Serrano, Uriel. 2020. "'Finding Home': Campus Racial Microclimates and Academic Homeplaces at a Hispanic-Serving Institution." *Race Ethnicity and Education,* 1–20.

Shukla, Pravina. 2005. "The Study of Dress and Adornment as Social Positioning." *Material Culture Review* 61 (1): 4–16.

Shukla, Pravina. 2008. *The Grace of Four Moons: Dress, Adornment, and the Art of the Body in Modern India*. Bloomington: Indiana University Press.

Shukla, Pravina. 2015. *Costume: Performing Identities through Dress*. Bloomington: Indiana University Press.

Shuman, Amy. 2005. Other People's Stories: *Entitlement Claims and the Critique of Empathy*. Urbana: University of Illinois Press.

Shuman, Amy, and Carol Bohmer. 2016. "The Stigmatized Vernacular: Political Asylum and the Politics of Visibility/Recognition." In *The Stigmatized Vernacular: Where Reflexivity Meets Untellability*, edited by Diane Goldstein and Amy Shuman, 90–117. Bloomington: Indiana University Press.

Silva, Jennifer M. 2012. "Constructing Adulthood in an Age of Uncertainty." *American Sociological Review* 77 (4): 505–522.

Silverstein, Michael, and Greg Urban, eds. 1996. *Natural Histories of Discourse*. Chicago: University of Chicago Press.

Simón, Yara. 2016. "9 Young Central American Creatives and Thought Leaders You Should Be Following." Remezcla. http://remezcla.com/lists/culture/central -american-creatives-and-thought-leaders-you-should-be-following/.

Sims, Martha. 2020. "Illness Tattoos: A Study of Embodied Traditions and Narratives." PhD diss., Ohio State University.

Skwarecki, Beth. 2017. "How to Make a Graduation Cap Fit on Kinky or Curly Hair." Life Hacker. May 3, 2017. https://www.lifehacker.com.au/2017/05/how-to-make-a -graduation-cap-fit-on-kinky-or-curly-hair/.

Slaughter, Stephany. 2016. "#TrumpEffects: Creating Rhetorical Spaces for Latinx Political Engagement." *Latin Americanist* 60 (4): 541–576.

Slocum-Bradley, Nikki. 2009. "The Positioning Diamond: A Trans-disciplinary Framework for Discourse Analysis." *Journal for the Theory of Social Behaviour* 40 (1): 79–107.

Solorzano, D., and T. Yosso. 2002. "Critical Race Methodology: Counter-Storytelling as an Analytical Framework for Education Research." *Qualitative Inquiry* 8 (1): 23–44.

"SpongeBob SquarePants." n.d. Encyclopedia SpongeBobia. https://spongebob.fandom .com/wiki/SpongeBob_SquarePants_(character)#Personality. Accessed October 7, 2021.

Stahl (Dolby), Sandra. 1977. "The Personal Narrative as Folklore." *Journal of the Folklore Institute* 14 (1/2): 9–30.

Stahl (Dolby), Sandra. 1989. *Literary Folkloristics and the Personal Narrative*. Bloomington: Indiana University Press.

Suárez-Orozco, Carola, and Marcelo M. Suárez-Orozco. 2001. *Children of Immigration*. Cambridge, MA: Harvard University Press.

Sutton-Smith, Brian. 1970. "Psychology of Childlore: The Triviality Barrier." *Western Folklore* 29 (1): 1–8.

Syeed, Esa. 2018. "Thinking Caps." *Contexts* 17 (2): 67–69. https://contexts.org/articles /thinking-caps/.

Syeed, Esa. 2020. "Wearing Many Hats: Students of Color and the Grounded Aesthetics of Graduation." *Journal of Diversity in Higher Education* 14 (3): 364–373.

Terkel, Studs. 1980. *American Dreams: Lost and Found*. New York: Pantheon Books.

Thompson, Chalmer E., and Bruce R. Fretz. 1991. "Predicting the Adjustment of Black College Students on a Predominantly White Campus." *Journal of Higher Education* 62 (4): 437–450.

Toelken, Barre. 1996. *Dynamics of Folklore*. Logan: Utah State University Press.

Torres, Heather. 2016. "Pride or Prejudice: Native Regalia and Graduation Ceremonies." Blogging Circle. July 6, 2016. https://bloggingcircle.wordpress.com/2016/07/06 /pride-or-prejudice-native-regalia-and-graduation-ceremonies/.

Trafzer, Clifford E., Jean A. Keller, and Lorene Sisquoc, eds. 2006. *Boarding School Blues: Revisiting American Indian Educational Experiences*. Lincoln: University of Nebraska Press.

Tsing, Anna Lowenhaupt. 2015. *The Mushroom at the End of the World: On the Possibility of Life in Capitalist Ruins*. Princeton, NJ: Princeton University Press.

UNLV Media Relations. 2017. "Spring 2017 Outstanding UNLV Graduates." UNLV News Center. https://www.unlv.edu/news/article/spring-2017-outstanding-unlv -graduates.

UNLV Media Relations. 2021. "Spring 2021 Outstanding UNLV Graduates." UNLV News Center. https://www.unlv.edu/news/article/spring-2021-outstanding-unlv -graduates.

Walters, Helen. 1939. *The Story of Caps and Gowns*. Chicago: E. R. Moore Company.

Wang, Frances Kai-Hwa. 2015. "Native Hawaiian Graduates Wearing Nothing but Cultural Pride." NBCNews. January 12, 2015. https://www.nbcnews.com/news/asian -america/native-hawaiian-graduates-wearing-nothing-cultural-pride-n284426.

Warner, Michael. 2002. "Publics and Counter Publics." *Public Culture* 14 (1): 49–90.

White, John Kenneth. 2016. "Whose Dream? US Presidents, Hispanics, and the Struggle for the American Future." In *The Latino/a American Dream*, edited by Sandra L. Hanson and John Kenneth White, 18–41. College Station: Texas A&M University Press.

Willsey, Kristiana. 2015. "Falling Out of Performance: Pragmatic Breakdown in Veteran's Storytelling." In *Diagnosing Folklore: Perspectives on Health, Trauma, and Disability*, edited by Trevor J. Blank and Andrea Kitta, 215–232. Jackson: University Press of Mississippi.

Wojcik, Daniel. 1995. *Punk and Neo-Tribal Body Art*. Jackson: University Press of Mississippi.

Yosso, T. J. 2005. "Whose Culture Has Capital? A Critical Race Theory Discussion of Community Cultural Wealth." *Race Ethnicity and Education* 8 (1): 69–91.

Zalaquett, Carlos P. 2006. "Study of Successful Latina/o Students." *Journal of Hispanic Higher Education* 5 (1): 35–47.

Index

Abad, Dr. Erika G., 102
academic achievement, 28, 55, 77, 87–88, 110, 119
Academic Council on Education (ACE), 65
academic dress, 11–13, 25–26, 65–66, 68, 74, 84–85, 94–95, 122*n16*
academic homeplace, 122*n3*
accumulation, 103
activism, 94–95
Adams, David Wallace, 124*n5*
Adams, James Truslow, 28
adulthood, transition from adolescence, 8, 18, 28, 102, 104–5
adulting, 104–6, 126*n1*
advice-giving narratives, 87
affiliations, social positioning, 20, 21*f*
affirmation of dominant cultural narratives, 117–18
African American graduates, 13, 73–74, 75*f*, 78, 124*n11*, 124*n12*
age theme, 14
Ahmed, Sara, 64
alternatives to success narratives, 106, 110
ambivalence theme, 98, 109
American dream, 17, 28, 80, 82–83, 89–92, 95, 96, 117
anecdotes, 126*n2*
anonymity of research participants, 121*n2*, 123*n7*
Anzaldúa, Gloria, 81, 102, 103, 125*n5*
Arab American graduates, 9
articulation of personal expression, 114
Asian/Asian American graduates, 9, 11, 23–24, 49–50
assimilation narrative, 71, 72, 82–83, 86, 89, 93*f*, 94–95, 123*n4*, 124*n5*, 124*n7*
audience: decorated mortarboards, 6, 100; family, 23, 32; material genre, 30; personal expression, 15; self-expression, 35

Bakhtin, Mikhail, 18, 35, 98
banning non-academic dress, 67, 68, 69, 70–72, 123*n3*
beading, 13, 67, 69, 70
Beatles, 56

Begay, Dawn, 72
believing theme, 32–34, 36*f*
belonging and exclusion: assimilation, 72, 124*n7*; Black hairstyles, 74, 75*f*; citizenship, 17; disruptive narratives, 93*f*, 95; dominant discourses, 84, 95; higher education, 30, 65, 117; Latino/a/x graduates, 83, 125*n5*; LGBTQ+ graduates, 65, 101, 117; marginalized graduates, 123*n1*, 123*n2*; official dress codes, 124*n11*; rhetorical reclamation, 65; social justice messaging, 40*f*, 79; students of color, 7, 78, 117; visibility, 77
Bettie, Julie, 125*n5*
Bible verses, 24, 43–46
biological deficit thinking, 86
birthdays, 122*n14*
boarding schools, Native American students, 71
Bohmer, Carol, 73
boundaries, significant, 113
Boven, David T., 66
Brayboy, Bryan McKinley Jones, 124*n5*, 124*n6*
Bronner, Simon, 26, 66, 96
Bruner, Jerome, 115
Bush, George W., 80
butterflies, immigrant theme, 54, 62, 81, 82*f*

calendar customs, 122*n14*
campus organizations, 24
Cann, Candi, 123*n8*
Cantú, Norma, 115, 126*n14*
cap and gown. *See* academic dress; mortarboards
carnivalesque, 98
Castro, Rafaela G., 125*n5*
celebration of space, 80, 97*f*
celebratory dancing/mood, 75, 123*n6*
cempasúchil, 32, 57
de Certeau, Michel, 107–8
change in social status, 96, 98
Chavez, Leo R., 83, 92
Chiang-López, Claudia, 125*n1*
Chicano/a students, 103, 124*n8*
children's media, 104–6, 113

chingona, 88, 125*n5*

Christensen, Danielle, 17, 108

Christmas, 122*n14*

Chumakov, 126*n10*

Cisneros, Sandra, 125*n5*

citizenship: American dream, 96, 117; belonging and exclusion, 17; dominant narratives, 85, 95; immigrants, 62, 83, 91, 92, 94

claiming space, 14, 114

class-based identities, 81

climate crisis, 113

clothing, symbolism, 122*n12*

Clothing Concepts, 12

collective meanings of decorations, 118

college degrees, 8, 50, 55, 87–88

college enrollment decline, 118–19

coming-of-age transitional period, 28, 104–5

commencement ceremonies: academic dress, 65–66, 96; change in social status, 96, 98; conventions, 64; COVID-19 pandemic, 121*n6*; decorated mortarboards, 55*f*; designated roles, 64; disruptive narrative, 95, 98; formality, 49, 67, 123*n3*; future-oriented messaging, 99*f*, 100–101; hierarchical roles, 96; institutional norms/values, 4, 64, 73; meaning, 112*f*; Native American identities, 71; neutrality, 67–68; personal adornment, 40*f*, 122*n8*; political protests, 79–80; self-expression, 34–35; sharing of oneself, 34; spatial hierarchy, 96; specialty, 124*n13*; undisciplining, 113; uniformity, 25–26, 67, 123*n3*; visual hierarchy, 96; walking, 39, 70, 88

communal narratives, 25, 44, 66, 113, 115, 118, 123*n4*, 124*n4*

conferral of degrees, 4

conformity of academic dress, 25–26, 73, 74

consejos, 87

contextualization, identity categories, 20

coping mechanisms, 39, 40

core values, American dream, 28, 64, 82–83, 89, 98

Costa Rica, 126*n9*

countertrivialization, 113

COVID-19 Pandemic, 118–19, 121*n6*

Coyolxauhqui Imperative, 102, 103*f*

creative expression, 18, 84

Critical Latinx Folkloristics, 83–84, 95

criticism of higher education, 27*f*, 79

Cruz Gomez, Brenda Carolina, 121*n5*, 125*n1*

cultural deficit thinking, 86, 87

cultural heritage: academic achievement, 87; American dream, 28, 82–83, 99; diversity, 69;

dominant, 103*f*, 104; higher education, 96–97; intersectionality, 84; Latino/a/x graduates, 83; narratives, 49, 89, 90*f*, 94; popular, 81; self-expression, 115; success, 28, 96–97, 110; rearticulation, 98; symbolism, 68–69; theme, 92, 94; undisciplining, 103–4; values, 17

DACA. *See* Deferred Action for Childhood Arrivals

dancing, celebratory, 75

data collection and analysis, 9, 11

debt, student loans, 7, 98

decision-making processes, 65

decontextualization, personal-experience narratives, 40–41, 116

decorated mortarboards. *See* mortarboards

Deferred Action for Childhood Arrivals (DACA), 31

deficit thinking, 86, 87*f*

Delgado-Gaitan, Concha, 125*n7*

demographics, political messaging, 91*f*

destabilization of power structures, 98

destigmatization, suicide, 57*f*

Development, Relief, and Education for Alien Minors Act. *See* DREAM Act

Día de Muertos theme, 32, 92

dialogic construction of self, 18, 35, 37, 89–90, 116–17, 122*n2*

dichos, 87*f*

differences, permissible display, 72–73

digital folklore genre: humor, 43*f*, 44, 106–7

digital public sphere. *See* social media

disabilities, students with, 7, 39

disciplinarity, higher education, 106

discipline, commencement ceremonies, 96

discursive references, 18, 113

display of difference, 72–73

disruptive narratives: assimilation, belonging, and exclusion, 93, 95; commencement ceremonies, 95, 98; graduation stage, 75–76, 95; low brow popular culture references, 44; marginalized communities, 95, 108–9; motifs, 111; students of color, 80–81, 95

diverse communities, data collection and analysis, 11

diversity, 11, 69, 72–73

domestic violence, 13

dominant cultural narratives: affirmation of, 117–18; alignment with, 117–18; American dream, 28, 83, 95; belonging and exclusion, 84, 95; citizenship, 85, 95; deficit thinking, 86, 87*f*; dress codes, 70; linearity, 48, 103*f*,

104; political dissent, 84, 95; rearticulation, 85, 95; resistance to, 72, 85, 90–91, 117–18; slogan-concepts, 115–16; societal power structures, 113; undisciplining, 103–4; whiteness, 124*n10*

Douglas, Mary, 124*n8*

Downs, Kristina, 113, 126*n2*

DREAM Act (Development, Relief, and Education for Alien Minors Act), 28*f*, 36*f*, 61, 81, 84–85, 89–90

dreaming theme, 32–34, 36*f*

dress codes, 11–12, 65–66, 70, 73–74, 75*f*, 96, 122*n9*, 122*n12*

Dundes, Alan, 15, 17, 99, 100

Dundes Renteln, Alison, 70

Dyer, Richard, 124*n10*

eagle feathers, 13, 67–69, 71, 72

employer requirements, college diploma, 8

empowerment, visibility, 76

engagement, public audiences, 56

enrollment, college, decline of, 118–19

equality, academic dress, 22–26, 66

Espinosa, Nicole Cristina, 125*n1*

ethnic names, mispronunciations, 74

ethnicity, 14, 40*f*, 71, 81

evaluation of decorated mortarboards, 54–55

Facebook, 4

faculty, 3, 7, 121*n4*

failure narrative, 105–6

family stories: audience, 23, 32; immigrants, 88; larger than personal, 23, 87–90; Latino/a/x graduates, 88; memorial theme, 24, 56; public audiences, 23, 88; recontextualization, 88; social media, 88

fandom communities, 25, 122*n17*

feminist activism messaging, 12–13, 38, 40*f*, 81, 88, 108, 122*n11*

financial hardship, 97*f*, 98

first-generation college students, 6, 11

Fivecoate, Jesse, 113, 126*n1*

flag imagery, 26*f*, 49, 59, 89, 90*f*, 91, 125*n8*

floral decorations, 27*f*, 32, 36*f*, 49, 59, 60, 62, 77*f*

folklore scholarship, 14, 29, 126*n3*

folk speech, 89, 126*n9*

folk traditions, 16, 93*f*, 113, 117

foregrounding messaging, 35, 99*f*, 100, 116

forgetting theme, 106–8

formality of commencement ceremonies, 49, 67, 123*n3*

formative experiences, 35

forward momentum/future-oriented messaging, 99*f*, 100–101, 103, 109*f*, 110

Fretz, Bruce R., 123*n1*

funding for education, 118–19

Game of Thrones, 97

Gatling, Benjamin, 126*n3*

gender, personal adornment, 14, 40*f*, 81

generic meanings, media intertextuality, 44

genetic deficit thinking, 86

geographical regions, 36

Germany, 23, 122*n16*

Goldstein, Diane, 115–16

González, Kenneth P., 123*n1*, 124*n8*

González-Martín, Rachel V., 75–76, 83–84, 92, 124*n7*, 125*n6*, 126*n14*

Good, Crystal, 124*n9*

Goodson, Christopher, 122*n1*

Google, 108

Gordon, Sarah M., 126*n3*

graduates: of color, 64; first-generation, 11; immigrant status, 54, 81, 82, 90, 91, 92, 94; influential people, 15–16; interpretation, 9–10; marginalization, 76; undocumented, 31–32, 51–53, 61, 81

graduation dress, 48–49, 51–53, 85

graduation stage, 75–76, 95

gratitude for parents, 81

haku lei, 49

Halberstam, Jack, 102, 103, 105, 106

Hamilton quotes, 53–54

Harrision, Albert A., 122*n8*

Harry Potter theme, 55

hashtags, 126*n15*

Hayden Griffith v. Caney Valley Public School District, 67–68, 70

Haynes, Deborah J., 35–36

Heath, Shirley Brice, 125*n7*

Hertz, Carrie, 48, 122*n9*, 122*n12*

heteronormativity, linear worldview, 101, 104

hierarchy of academic dress, 11–12, 66, 96

higher education: American dream, 17, 28, 80, 117; attitudes, 8–9; belonging and exclusion, 30, 65, 117; core values, 64, 98; criticism, 27*f*, 79; cultural narratives, 96–97; disciplinarity, 106; diversity, 11; inequality, 79; institutional affirmation, 109; knowledge and expertise, 96; policies, 5; purpose, 17, 64, 66; racism, 78; status, 96, 98; structural inequalities, 77–78; value of, 7*f*, 8, 9, 64, 98, 118–19

Hispanic graduates. *See* Latino/a/x graduates
historias familias. *See* family stories
hobby theme, 32–34
holidays, 122*n14*
homeplace, academic, 122*n3*
honor chords, 12, 69
hooding ceremony, 3
hooks, bell, 122*n3*
Horigan, Kate Parker, 17, 122*n3*
Huffman Walker, Lauren, 65, 66
human-animal relationships, 21, 22*f*, 34, 122*n13*
humor, 5, 6, 97*f*, 98; ambivalent laughter, 97*f*,
    98; coping mechanism, 39, 40; Internet
    memes, 39, 40, 43–44, 106–7; occupational,
    16; popular culture references, 98; public
    audiences, 43–44, 106–7; self-expression, 37;
    wordplay, 16
hyperdocumentation, 85–86
hypervisibility, Black hairstyles, 73, 75*f*

"I have 3 dollars" meme, 97*f*, 98
ICE [Immigration and Customs
    Enforcement], 51, 52, 53
identity, self/community, 19*f*, 20, 65, 113
illness tattoos, 123*n8*
illuminated manuscripts, 111, 112, 118
image macros, 43*f*
immigrants: academic achievement, 55,
    87–88; citizenship, 62, 83, 90, 91, 92, 94;
    college degrees, 54, 55, 62, 82–83, 87–88;
    Latinidad, 125*n2*; messaging, 32, 54, 85, 86,
    91*f*; political movement, 62, 81, 82*f*, 90, 92;
    stereotypes, 85; undocumented and unafraid
    movement, 92
impersonalization/personalization, 114
inclusion, community-building, 44, 66
individual identities: larger community experi-
    ence, 44, 89–90, 115; material genre, 30;
    narratives, 115–16; performance genre, 30;
    self-expression, 20, 28, 99, 115; success, 116;
    symbolism, 118
indoctrination, perception of, 7, 121*n4*
inequality, social justice messaging, 40*f*, 79–80
influential people, 15–16, 18
inside jokes, 42
inspirational quotes, 15, 16*f*, 81
Instagram, 4
institutional narratives: commencement
    ceremonies, 64, 73; graduates of color, 64;
    higher education, 109; performance genre,
    123*n4*, 124*n4*; rearticulation, 98; rite of
    intensification, 64; whiteness, 64

integration of school colors, 123*n4*, 124*n4*
Interdisciplinary Studies, 6, 121*n3*
Internet memes, 39, 40, 43–44, 78, 89, 106–7
interpretations of personal narratives, 9–10,
    17
intersectionality, 44, 84, 118
intertextuality in media, 40–41, 106, 117
interview participants, 8, 9, 10, 121*n2*, 121*n7*
irreverence, 98
Ivey, Bill, 5

jewelry decorations, 46, 49
Joseph, Penial E., 126*n12*

Kahlo, Frida, 60, 61, 81
Kapchan, Deborah, 3, 30
Keaton, Kevin, 122*n10*
Kelley, Greg, 111, 124*n5*
kente stoles, 13
Kiyama, Judy Marquez, 125*n7*
know-your-place aggression, 124*n14*

larger than personal narratives, 17, 21, 23, 25,
    88–90, 92, 116–18
LaRocque, SaNoah, 72
Latina Rebels, 80–81, 86, 88, 92, 114
Latinidad, 80, 81, 84, 93, 125*n2*
Latino/a/x graduates: academic achievement,
    87–88; American dream, 83, 89, 90, 91, 92;
    assimilation, 86, 89; belonging, 83, 125*n5*;
    cultural citizenship, 83; decorated mortar-
    boards, 125*n1*; deficit thinking, 86, 87*f*; fam-
    ily stories, 88; graduates, 9, 81; larger than
    personal experiences, 92; Latino threat nar-
    rative, 83, 91, 92; LGBTQ+, 125*n4*; popular
    culture references, 92, 93*f*; private/public
    spheres, 83–84; resistance, 77*f*, 89, 90–91;
    self-documentation, 93; serape scarves, 13;
    "Sí se puede!," 90, 126*n11*; social justice
    messaging, 79, 81; social media, 29; struggle
    and resilience theme, 90; symbolism, 40;
    walking across the stage, 75–76
#LatinxGradCaps hashtag, 18, 80–81, 85–87,
    89, 90, 92–95, 114
legal actions, traditional dress bans, 68–69,
    71, 72
leis, 13, 23, 49–50
#LetTheFeathersFly hashtag, 72
Levi, Mary, 71
LGBTQ+, 122*n10*; belonging, 65, 101, 117;
    flowers, 59; Latinx community, 125*n4*; rain-
    bow imagery, 59; 63, re-membering, 103,

104; resilience, 102; trans flag, 18, 122*n10*; visibility, 60–62

liberal arts colleges, 10

life experiences, 41–42

linear worldview, 48, 101, 102, 103*f,* 104

linguistic deficit thinking, 86

Lomawaima, K. Tsianina, 124*n5*

Loo, Chalsa M., 123*n1*

low-brow popular culture references, 44, 113

low theory, 105–6

Lowenhaupt Tsing, Anna, 108–9

maile, 13

Maldonado, Marta María, 125*n7*

malo, 13

Manning, Kathleen, 6, 97

manuscripts, illuminated, 111, 112, 118

Maraj, Louis M., 65, 124*n11*

marginalized student communities, 65, 71, 76, 77*f,* 84, 94, 95, 113

Marrun, Norma, 87–88, 123*n4*

Martínez, Elena, 125*n8*

mascots, stereotypes, 68

mass media texts, 40–42, 43, 44, 106–7

master's degrees (MA/MS/MSW), 3, 9

material genre: audience, 30; meanings, 14, 30, 36, 112; protest signs, 80; scrapbooks, 17, 35; social identities, 30, 40

Matos, J.M.D., 125*n7*

McCarty, Teresa L., 124*n5*

McGriff, Meredith, 113, 126*n2*

McNeill, Lynne, 126*n15*

meanings: collective, 118; illuminated manuscripts, 111, 112, 118; material genre, 14, 30, 36*f,* 112*f;* wedding dresses, 122*n9. See also* symbolism

media intertextuality, 40–42, 43, 44, 106–7

Meheula, Barbara, 13

memes on social media platforms, 39, 40, 44, 89, 97, 98, 106–7

memorial theme, 24, 56

mental health issues, 39, 40, 57*f,* 58–59, 62

Mexican identity, 49, 77, 89, 91, 93, 94–95

milestones, linear worldview, 48, 101, 102, 104

military service theme, 26*f,* 49, 50*f*

Minaj, Nicki, 41, 42*f*

minority-serving institutions, 10, 11

Miranda, Carmen, 60, 62

Mitchell, Koritha, 124*n14*

Mojica Rodríguez, Prisca Dorcas, 80–81, 92

Monette, Melvin, 68

mortarboards, decorated: ambivalence, 98, 109; beading, 13, 67, 69, 70; believing theme, 32–34, 36; Bible verses, 24, 43–46; Black hairstyles, 74, 75; butterflies, 54, 62, 81, 82, 62; *cempasúchil,* 32, 57; dreaming theme, 32–34, 36; eagle feathers, 13, 67–69, 71, 72; flags, 26*f,* 49, 59, 89, 90*f,* 91, 125*n8;* flowers, 27*f,* 32, 36*f,* 49, 59, 60, 62, 77*f;* hobbies, 32–34; jewelry, 46, 49; military service, 26*f,* 49, 50*f;* origins, 65; popularity, 15, 16, 34, 121*n1,* 121*n5;* process of decorating, 21–23, 122*n15,* 122*n16;* quotes, 53, 108; social media, 55, 80; symbolism, 11–12, 68–69, 85, 122*n9,* 122*n12,* 125*n8;* triviality barrier, 112. *See also* humor

Mother's Day, 122*n14*

motifs, disruptive point of view, 111

motivation of graduates, 9–10

Multidisciplinary Studies degree, 121*n3*

multifaceted identities, 20

multiple decorated mortarboards, 55*f*

multiple personal narratives, 40*f*

Muñoz, Susana María, 125*n7*

My Favorite Murder, 25, 122*n17*

names, mispronunciation, 38, 74, 123*n4*

narcissism, selfie culture, 126*n2*

narrative scholarship, 20

Nathan, Rebekah, 25

national identity, 14, 89, 90*f*

Native American graduates: assimilation, 71, 72, 124*n5;* ban compromise, 70–72; beaded caps, 69; eagle feathers, 72; stereotypes, 68; traditional dress, 13, 66–67, 71; visibility, 72

Native Hawaiian graduates, 9, 13, 23, 49–50

#NativeLivesMatter, 72

neutrality, 67–68

Nevada, Las Vegas, University of. *See* UNLV

news coverage, 10

no adornment policies. *See* banning non-academic dress

nontraditional students, 6, 32–34, 101, 104

Noyes, Dorothy, 116, 126*n2*

Obama, Barack, 126*n11*

obstacles, foregrounding, 100

occupational humor, 16

official dress codes, belonging and exclusion, 124*n11*

Ohio State University, The, 3, 10, 21, 22*f,* 33, 75*f*

older graduates, 7, 32–34

de Onís, Catalina (Kathleen) M., 125*n4*
online survey research method, 9
originality, self-expression, 55–56
origins of academic dress, 65
outsider judgment, cultural expression, 84
Oversen, Kylie, 69

Pacific Islander graduates, 9, 11, 23
Pagter, Carl, 15–17
parental gratitude/inspiration, 81, 93
Paz, Octavio, 125*n5*
Perez, Domino Renee, 115
performance genre: community narrative, 44,
    123*n4*, 124*n4*; disruptive point of view, 111;
    illuminated manuscripts, 111, 118; individual
    identities, 30; institutional narrative, 123*n4*,
    124*n4*; material genre, 9, 30; nature of, 15;
    performance of self, 55–56; self-expression,
    114–15; social identities, 30
performative/personal decision-making pro-
    cesses, 65
permissible display of differences, 72–73
Perry, Andre, 73
personal adornment, 13–14, 36, 40*f*, 122*n8*,
    122*n9*
personal experience narratives: anecdotes,
    126*n2*; articulation, 114; audience, 15; claim-
    ing space, 114; community, 25; conventions,
    17; decontextualization, 116; identities,
    26*f*; interpretations, 17; intersectionality,
    118; larger than personal, 89–90, 116–18;
    Latino/a/x graduates, 92; media discourse,
    41; political expression, 40*f*, 89–90, 114;
    popular culture references, 41; public audi-
    ences, 17, 40*f*, 41; recontextualization, 17,
    116; scrapbooks, 17; significance, 114; trivi-
    alization, 114, 126*n2*; valorization, 116
personalization/impersonalization, academic
    dress, 12–13, 56, 114
Peterson, Mark Allen, 40–41, 43
pets, human-animal relationships, 21, 22*f*, 34,
    122*n13*
physical space of commencement ceremonies,
    64
Pineda, Richard D., 125*n8*
Pinterest, 4
Platt, R. Eric, 65, 66
political messaging, 5–6, 88–89, 121*n4*; aca-
    demic dress, 12–13; acts of resistance, 20,
    72, 90–91, 117–18; articulation, 114; celebra-
    tion of space, 80; commencement ceremo-
    nies, 79–80; demographics, 91; dominant

discourses, 84, 95; immigrants' rights, 32,
    54, 61, 84–85, 89–90, 91, 92, 94; oppression,
    19, 20; personal expression, 40, 89–90, 114;
    punk culture, 47, 48; self-expression, 20
political views, faculty, 7, 121*n4*
popular cultural references, 81; disruptive
    messaging, 44; fandom communities, 25;
    humor, 98; Latino/a/x graduates, 92, 93;
    material performance, 40; personal experi-
    ences, 41; popular sayings, 87; television, 43
popularity of decorated mortarboards, 4, 15,
    16*f*, 34, 121*n1*, 121*n5*
positioning, social, 20, 20, 21*f*
power structures, 98, 113
precarity theme, 109*f*, 110
presentation of colors, 4
preserving traditions, 68, 72
prevalence of decorated mortarboards, 121*n1*,
    121*n5*
primarily white colleges/universities, 10
private spheres, Latino/a/x communities,
    83–84
process of decorating mortarboards, 23,
    122*n15*, 122*n16*
process of trivialization, 113
procession, graduates, 3
procrastination theme, 108–9
promoting cultural diversity, 69
protest signs, 80, 122*n11*
proverbs, 15, 87, 89
public audiences: digital folklore genre, 43;
    engagement, 56; family stories, 23, 88;
    humor, 43–44, 106–7; inside jokes, 42; per-
    sonal narratives, 17, 41; social media, 55;
    visibility, 60–62
public funding for education, 118–19
public spheres, Latino/a/x communities, 83–84
Puerto Rican culture, 125*n8*
punk culture theme, 47, 48*f*, 51, 123*n8*
purpose of higher education, 17, 64, 66

quantitative research methods, 10, 122*n8*
queer temporalities, 102
quinceañera celebrations, 124*n7*, 125*n6*
Quintanilla-Pérez, Selena, 92–93
quotes, inspirational, 53, 81, 108

Rabelais, François, 98
racial injustice theme, 14, 18, 19*f*, 20, 40*f*, 78,
    79, 91, 113
rainbow flag, 59, 63
raised fist imagery, 18, 90–91, 126*n12*

reaffirmation, ritual performance, 98

rearticulation of dominant narratives, 29, 85, 95, 98

recontextualization: children's media, 106; family stories, 88; intertextuality, 40–41; personal narratives, 17, 116

region, 14, 36

relational self-expression, 17, 20, 21*f*, 34–35, 40*f*

religious symbolism, 14, 24, 43–46, 68–69

re-membering, 102, 103*f*, 104

Remezcla, Estaff, 125*n3*

research methods, 8, 9, 10, 11, 122*n8*, 123*n7*

resilience theme, 94, 102, 116

resistance to dominant narratives, 20, 27*f*, 72, 76, 77*f*, 85, 90–91, 94–95, 117–18

#ResistCulturalGenocide, 72

reversing traditional dress bans, 69, 72

rhetoric, undocumented graduates, 51–53, 61, 122*n1*

rhetorical reclamation, 65, 79

Rice, Condoleezza, 80

right of intensification, 8

Rios-Aguilar, Cecilia, 125*n7*

rites of passage, 8, 11–12, 64, 122*n9*

ritual space of commencement ceremonies, 34–35, 65–66

Rolison, Garry, 123*n1*

Rosencranz, Mary Lou, 12

Rowling, J.K., 55

sacrifice theme, 88

Saenz, Benjamin, 53

Sawin, Patricia, 122*n2*

scatological imagery, 98

scholarship/research, 10, 20, 29, 122*n8*

school colors, integration, 123*n4*, 124*n4*

scrapbooks, 17, 108

Sebron, Ginai, 124*n12*

Sedlacek, William E., 123*n1*

self, dialogic construction, 18, 37, 122*n2*

self-documentation, Latino/a/x graduates, 93

self-expression: audience, 35; cultural function, 115; foregrounding, 35; graduation dress, 48–49; humor, 37; identity, 113; individual function, 20, 115; material genre, 30; originality, 55–56; performance genre, 114–15; personal adornment, 14, 40*f*, 114; political messaging, 20; popular culture references, 40; relational, 20, 21*f*, 34–35; re-membering, 103; ritual space of commencement ceremonies, 34–35; space, claiming, 14; traditional forms, 15

selfie culture, 126*n2*

serape scarves, 13

Serebriany, Zoey, 71

Serrano, Uriel, 122*n3*

service dog, 21, 22*f*

shared experiences of marginalized communities, 94

Shukla, Pravina, 20, 49, 50–51

Shuman, Amy, 73, 116–17

"¡Sí Se Pudo!: The Art and Stories of Latinx Graduation Caps," 125*n1*

"¡Sí, se pudo!"/"¡Sí se puede!," 90, 91*f*, 126*n11*

significance of messaging, 112–14

Silva, Jennifer M., 102

Sims, Martha, 123*n8*

Sisquoc, Lorene, 124*n5*

situated knowledge, 116–17

slogan-concepts, 116

snowball sampling, 9

Snyder, Rick, 80

social expression, personal expression, 17, 40*f*

social identities, material genre, 30

social justice messaging, 40*f*, 79–81, 91

social media: community building, 44; decorated mortarboards, 55, 80; family stories, 88; immigrants, 85; Internet memes, 39, 40, 44, 78, 106–7; Latino/a/x communities, 18, 29, 81, 86, 92; memes, 44, 97, 98, 106–7; popularity in decorated mortarboards, 4; public audiences, 55; racism, 94; research method, 8

social positioning, 20, 21*f*

Social Science Studies degree, 121*n3*

social status, 13–14, 96, 98, 113

solidarity, mental health issues, 57*f*

Solorzano, Daniel G., 125*n7*

song lyrics, 23, 24, 41–42, 56

Sowards, Stacey K., 125*n8*

space of commencement, 14, 64, 65, 113, 114

Spanish-language messaging, 24, 25, 32, 36*f*, 62, 92, 95

spatial hierarchy of commencement ceremonies, 96

speciality commencement ceremonies, 124*n13*

SpongeBob SquarePants, 97*f*, 98, 104–6, 107*f*

Stahl (Dolby), Sandra, 17

standardization of academic dress, 65–66

stereotypes, 68, 85

stigma of hypervisibility, 73

storytelling, 20

straight time, 101, 102, 103*f*, 104

strategies of students, 108

structural inequalities in higher education, 77–78

struggle and resilience theme, 89, 90, 123*n5*

student debt, 7, 97*f*, 98

student strategies and tactics, 108

students of color, 9–10, 121*n7*; assimilation, 38, 72, 123*n4*; belonging and exclusion, 7, 65, 78, 117; disruptive messaging, 80–81, 95; immigrants, 82–83; mispronunciation of names, 38, 123*n4*; visibility, 77

study participants, 9, 10, 121*n2*, 121*n7*

Suárez-Orozco, Carola and Marcelo, 82–83

success narrative: academic achievement, 28, 77, 110, 119; adulting, 105–6; alternatives, 106, 110; conventions, 17, 28, 102, 105–6, 110; cultural narrative, 28, 96–97, 110; individual responsibility, 116; visibility, 86, 110

suicide, destigmatization, 57*f*, 58–59

survey research method, 8, 9, 10

Syeed, Esa, 25, 76, 121*n7*, 123*n2*

symbolism: academic dress, 11–12; clothing, 122*n9*, 122*n12*; culture, 68–69; flags, 125*n8*; Hispanic graduates, 40; mortarboards, 85; religion, 44–45, 68–69

tactical nature of forgetting, 107–8

tattoos, 14, 35, 123*n9*

temporal progression, linear worldview, 101, 104

testimonios, 115

textual forms: discursive references, 18; material genre, 14, 36*f*; popular culture references, 40; struggle and resilience theme, 89, 90; transition to adulthood, 28, 104–5

Thomas, Bettyanne, 72

Thompson, Chalmer E., 123*n1*

Toelken, Barre, 100–101

Torres, Heather, 71

traditional dress, 13, 23, 49–50, 66–67, 70–72

Trafzer, Clifford E., 124*n5*

trans flag, 18, 122*n10*

transition to adulthood, 18, 28, 102, 104–5

triviality barrier, 112, 113, 114, 126*n2*

trucha, 91, 126*n13*

Trump, Donald, 5, 6, 80, 91

undergraduates, 3, 11, 12, 25, 29, 102, 121*n3*

undisciplining commencement ceremonies, 98, 103–4, 113

undocumented graduates, 31–32, 81; DREAM Act, 61, 84–85; graduation dress, 51–53, 85; hyperdocumentation, 85–86; political movements, 61, 84–85, 92; research participants, 121*n2*; rhetoric, 51–53, 61, 122*n1*; social media, 85; undocugrad ceremonies, 85, 122*n1*, 124*n13*; UndocuMedia and Define American, 85

uniformity of commencement ceremonies, 25–26, 29, 67, 69, 70, 73, 74, 123*n3*

uniqueness of self-expression, 11, 12, 14, 34, 36–37, 104, 115

United States flag, 26*f*, 49, 89

UNLV (University of Nevada, Las Vegas), 3, 6, 11, 22, 80, 101, 104, 121*n3*, 125*n1*

upward mobility, American dream, 28, 76, 84

valorization of personal-experience narratives, 6, 116

value of higher education, 6–9, 64, 98, 118–19

vernacular narratives, 11, 14, 100, 126*n2*

visibility: acceptable differences, 70, 73; Black hairstyles, 74, 75; *compasúchil*, 32, 57; empowerment, 76; kente stoles, 13; Latino/a/x graduates, 92; LGBTQ+, 60–62; marginalized students, 77; Native American dress, 71, 72; public audience, 60–62; success, 86, 110

visual forms of material genre, 13, 14, 18, 21, 29, 36*f*, 40, 43, 78, 89, 90, 103*f*, 104, 125*n8*

walking in commencement ceremonies, 24, 26, 39, 47, 59, 61, 70, 76, 88, 102

Warner, Michael, 84

weddings, 122*n9*, 122*n14*

white-centered narratives, 4, 9, 64, 73, 82–83, 91, 92, 124*n10*

Willsey, Kristiana, 17

Wojcik, Daniel, 123*n8*

women's rights, 122*n11*, 122*n15*

womxn, 80, 81

wordplay, 15–16

wrapping paper and bows, 121*n1*

written consent, study participants, 121*n2*

xenophobia, social justice messaging, 40*f*, 79, 91

Yosso, Tara J., 125*n7*

Zalaquett, Carlos P., 125*n7*

About the Author

SHEILA BOCK is associate professor in the Department of Interdisciplinary, Gender, and Ethnic Studies at the University of Nevada, Las Vegas.